A Boy from Wannaska

A Boy from Wannaska

ꟹ

Growing Up in Northern Minnesota 1915–1945

ꟹ

Marjorie Wright Mortensen

Family histories and stories
as first told by Ray Mortensen

Jugum Press

Originally published by the author as
"Ray's Stories: Stories told by Ray Mortensen
about family and neighbors in Wannaska, Minnesota"

Second Edition: November 2013
ISBN 978-1-939423-09-2

Published by Jugum Press
www.jugumpress.com

Editing, footnotes, and design:
Annie Pearson, with Martha Emily Pearson, Jugum Press
Cover design by LisaTiltonDesign

Credits:
All photos from family photo collection of Ray Mortensen

Contents

Foreword ... 7

I: EARLY WANNASKA LIFE ... 9

1: Finding Wannaska ... 11
- Natives, Trappers, Pioneers and Homesteaders in Roseau County ... 12
- Northern Europeans Come to Northern Minnesota ... 13

2: Coming to Wannaska ... 15
- Jens Mortensen in Denmark ... 15
- Jens and Ellen Mortensen Emigrate ... 17
- Jens and Ellen Mortensen in Iowa ... 21
- The Mortensen Family Moves to Roseau County ... 23
- Jens Olson Comes from Norway ... 27
- Jens and Ellen Mortensen in Wannaska ... 32

3: Early Days in Wannaska ... 35
- The Old-Timers Describe Early Life ... 35
- Native Americans of the Wannaska Area ... 36
- "If You Can't Find It at Lee's Store..." ... 38
- Other Businesses in Wannaska ... 41
- Stories from the Wannaska Old Timers ... 41

4: Wannaska School, Church, and Social Life ... 51
- Wannaska School Days ... 51
- Riverside Lutheran Church at Wannaska ... 56
- Social Life in Wannaska ... 60

II: MORTENSEN FAMILY AND FARM LIFE ... 69

5: Life on the Mortensen Farm ... 71
- Farm Work through the Seasons ... 72
- Andrew's Principles ... 86
- The Farm Animals ... 88
- Working Days at the Farm ... 90
- Hard Times in the 1930s ... 94
- Grandpa Mortensen Moves Back to the Farm ... 98

6: Mortensen and Sorter-Olson Families ... 101
- Stories of the Andrew and Julia Mortensen Family ... 101
- Stories of the Sorter-Olson Family ... 114

7: Mortensen Families in Later Years ... 119
- The Knudt and Annie Mortensen Lee Family ... 120
- The Clarence and Martha Mortensen Davis Family ... 121
- The Morten and Hilda Oslund Mortensen Family ... 121

The George and Christena Mortensen Johnson Family 124
The Chris Hardland and Hannah Mortensen Hardland Family 125
The Jens and Nettie Reed Mortensen Family 126
The Blanchard and Marie Mortensen Hunking Family 130
The Andrew Mortensen Family 131
APPENDIX 134
Mortensen-Olson Family History 134
The Children of Jens and Ellen Mortensen 138
About the Author 148
About Jugum Press 149

ꝏ

Foreword

From the Author - 1996

"I'm from Portland, Oregon. Where are you from?" I asked the soldier sitting beside me in a restaurant in Jackson, Michigan, May 8, 1943.

"Wannaska, Minnesota," he said.

"Where in the world is Wannaska?"

"Way up in the northwest corner of Minnesota," the soldier replied.

ꝏ

That was my introduction to Ray Mortensen and a way of life different from any I'd known.

During the years that followed, I repeatedly heard stories of a unique people living in a small isolated community. They were immigrants, mainly from Scandinavia, who "proved" homestead land, struggled to make a living on their farms, raised their families, built churches and schools, learned to become American citizens, and did everything else that went on in pioneer times.

These are some of the stories Ray told over the fifty years we had together. These stories are written to be passed lovingly on to our children and grandchildren. I hope they reveal the love he had for his family and his neighbors, and show the pride he had in their overcoming the hardships they endured to become the backbone of Roseau County, Minnesota.

The old-time Native Americans, the trappers, the homesteaders, and the settlers are all gone now. Ray's grandparents, his parents, all the aunts and uncles, and some cousins are gone also. Ray's sister Ardythe died in 1968, and Ray himself in 1993.

Information about the pre-history of Roseau County was obtained from the forward written by Hazel Walber, in the *Roseau County Heritage* book, published by the Roseau County Historical Society in 1992. Stories of the origin of Roseau County towns were obtained from the

County of Roseau Centennial book published in 1994 by the Roseau County Historical Society.

Another source of information was the genealogy report Mildred Mortensen Simmons wrote in 1982, "The Family of Jens and Marie Mortensen." Orval Mortensen supplied names for pictures and dates of some happenings.

Tussen Takk.

– Marjorie Mortensen, 1996

From the Editors - 2010, 2013

As the children of Ray and Marjorie Mortensen, we heard these stories over the dinner table or over cups of coffee while visiting with our father's brothers, sisters, and cousins.

After losing Ray in 1993, Marjorie set about to capture these stories. She wrote from her own memory and checked details with Ray's siblings. She consulted with sources from Wannaska and Roseau history where she could find them—but this was before the growth of the Internet and online information such as the Ellis Island records.

We doubled-checked Marjorie's efforts where we could online. However, this information is offered as a second-hand oral history—it's the history of a boy growing up in northern Minnesota during a time of great cultural and technological change, telling the story of first-generation rural immigrants building a new society and transitioning their farming practices to steam- and gasoline-powered machines.

This history captures, in our mother's and father's voices, the connection we had with an earlier generation of cousins and great-grandparents whom we never met, but who were with us every day in the stories we begged to be told and retold.

– The editors:
Annie Pearson
(daughter of Ray Mortensen)
Emily Pearson
(great-great-grandchild of Jens and Ellen Mortensen)

I: Early Wannaska Life

Lee's Store, Wannaska, 1906

℘

1: Finding Wannaska

Glaciers played a great part in forming the land of Manitoba and Saskatchewan in Canada, Minnesota, the Dakotas, and northwest Wisconsin. The glaciers left large gravel deposits, swamp land, deep peat deposits, and some very rocky ground besides good farming land.

In pioneer times, when rocky fields were cleared, more rocks rose to the surface because of the yearly freezing and thawing. The glaciers also scoured out innumerable lakes. Minnesota isn't called the "Land of 10,000 Lakes" for no reason.[1]

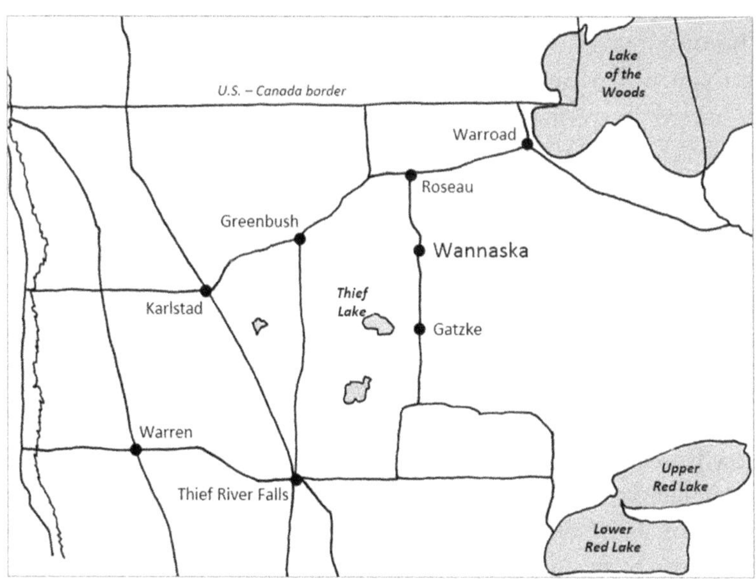

Wannaska, in Roseau County

Wannaska is on the south branch of the Roseau River, which flows north to the main branch of that river, then northwesterly to the Red River (of the North), continuing northerly into Lake Winnipeg. From there, the water flows into Hayes River and then into Hudson Bay.

---

[1] See Roseau County Geologic Map at http://reflections.mndigital.org/cdm/singleitem/collection/mgs/id/773

Natives, Trappers, Pioneers and Homesteaders in Roseau County

Several hundred years ago, Sioux tribes occupied most of this territory. Around 1700 they were replaced, unwillingly, by the Ojibwa or Chippewa tribes.

According to the records of the Hudson Bay Company, in 1732 French-Canadian voyagers crossed the Lake of the Woods into what is now Roseau (pronounced "Rose-o") County, Minnesota, to establish trading posts to gather and transport furs back to Montreal. In 1824 two fur-trading posts were established. One was at the mouth of the Warroad River, now the site of the town of Warroad, so named because it lies on the trail Native Americans used to travel to make war on their enemies.

The other post established was on the Roseau River, now the site of the town of Roseau and seat of the county of the same name. This town, settled by pioneers in 1887, is located 10 miles south of the Canadian border, 21 miles west of the Lake of the Woods and the town of Warroad, and 17 miles north of the town of Wannaska.

In Roseau County, some of the land differed greatly from that of the central plains areas of Iowa, Kansas, Nebraska, and the Dakotas. There were some very rocky areas, sand ridges, sticky "gumbo" and heavy soil, and quite a lot of swamp areas caused by working beavers. Although the area has much good grain-growing land, some was better as pasture and hay land.

> **How Roseau County Got Its Name:** This county, which was established December 31, 1894, takes its name from the Roseau lake and river. This lake, like many others in the state, derived its name from an Indian descriptive term. Although the name "Roseau" is taken from a French, it is a translation of the Ojibwa "Gashaggunushkawiskbl," meaning the place of the rushes river, first called this by French trappers.
>
> –From *Roseau-Times Region*, March 9, 1928
> submitted by Hazel Walberg

The pioneers faced other obstacles. Winters were severe. Especially after a wet spring, summer brought swarms of mosquitoes, bull flies, and ticks day and night. But in summer there was a good supply of small fruits, including blueberries, strawberries, June berries, and high-bush cranberries, all small in size but eagerly sought after by settlers.

Fish were plentiful as were deer, elk, moose, rabbits, and bear, all of which were welcomed by the pioneers.

Most of the land was heavily forested with spruce, birch, elm, and poplar trees, which were difficult to clear, but provided materials for building and heating the homes the settlers erected. Money was scarce and transportation was primitive, making the importing of supplies and exporting crops difficult, but in spite of these difficulties, the pioneers still came.

Minnesota became a state in 1857. In 1862 President Lincoln signed the Homestead Act, which granted 160 acres of land free to anyone who staked out a claim. In order for settlers to receive clear title, the land had to be cleared for planting of crops and a home had to be built within a certain number of years. Most of the land west of the Mississippi River was affected. As a result of this Act, settlers moved west in great numbers. Roseau County in northern Minnesota had some of the last available homestead land. In 1885 there were four settlers in Roseau County. More pioneers trekked in, and by 1889 there were about 600. James Jester filed for the first homestead claim in Roseau County, but numerous squatters had taken possession of land before that.

Northern Europeans Come to Northern Minnesota

Coinciding with the opening of homestead land, there was a great outpouring of emigrants from Europe, due mainly to poor economic and social conditions that threatened many with starvation. Into this land came Norwegians, Danes, Swedes, Poles, Germans, Bohemians, and others, some of them the poorest of the poor, but eager to take advantage of the opportunity of land, free for the proving. They built homes, churches, and schools and started businesses.

These immigrants did not always find the dream-land they may have envisioned, but they were free to become what they could by their own hard work, in spite of the difficulties. These new citizens treasured their new freedom greatly. If some voiced disappointment with their circumstances, eventually they'd be told, "The boat goes both ways, you know." Not very many went back to stay.

Some of the immigrants' stories revealed extreme hardship in the "Old Country." Mrs. Oslund, discussing salvation with Julia Mortensen, said that she didn't expect she'd go to Heaven when she died, because she could not forgive the Swedish farmer who chased her and her mother out of his potato field after harvest, where they'd been gleaning potatoes the size of marbles. They lived on bread made from tree bark. Other immigrants had similar stories; life in Europe was difficult for the poorer classes.

From the time the Homestead Act was signed until well after the turn of the twentieth century, settlers continued to come into northern Minnesota. Each year a new township was formed, a store started, a post office installed, a school district formed, and a school built. A church congregation was organized and then a church built. According to need, other small businesses such as a creamery and a blacksmith shop would be started. In some towns, a bank and a newspaper would be launched. This was how northern Minnesota was organized.

Most of the counties were large in area, and transportation was limited to horseback or horse and buggy over dirt roads. These roads became hard to travel on during the wet and snow seasons. Because of this difficulty, the counties were divided into smaller portions called "townships." Officials, elected locally, had responsibility for local road upkeep and school administration. They also had charged of elections.

During this time, a few of the towns settled were Roseau, Badger, Gatzke, Greenbush, Grygla, Leo, Malung, Middle River, Pelan, Pencer, Pine Creek, Rainie, Ross, Roosevelt (after Theodore), Salol, Strathcona, and Wannaska.

Wannaska is in Mickinock Township, named after a leader of the local Native American tribe.

2: Coming to Wannaska

Grandpa Jens Mortensen

Jens Mortensen in Denmark

Jens Mortensen, Ray's grandfather, was born to Morten and Johanna Mortensen in 1851 at Afjmyds Mans in Afjmyds County Northern District, Denmark.[2]

Morten's family had been wealthy landowners on a large island, but the oldest brother drank and gambled away their inheritance. Grandpa,

[2] See the genealogy of Jens and Ellen Mortensen in the appendix.

his father, mother, brothers and sisters moved to Fyn Island.[3] The father had never had to do manual labor, so he had no trade and could not feed his family. The children were sold as indentured servants; at least they'd be fed.

An indentured servant agreed to work for a certain length of time and had to endure any kind of treatment for that time if the person wanted to obtain a letter of discharge. The person could not leave to find another place to work, because no one would hire him without a letter of discharge.

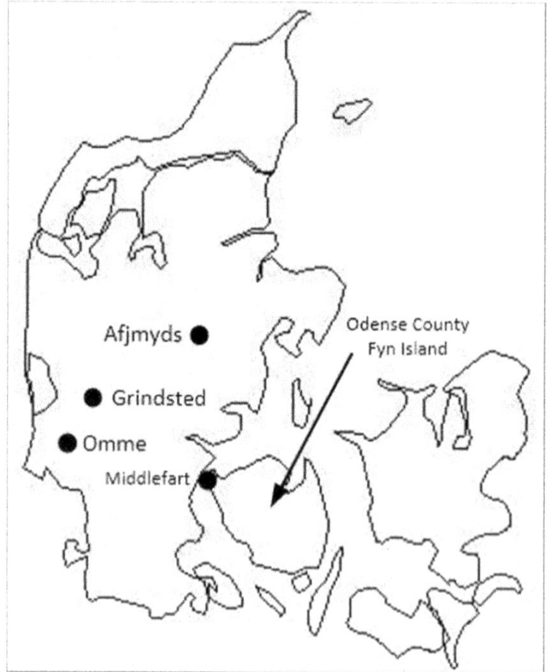

Mortensen Home Counties in Denmark

Jens Mortensen—later called "Grandpa" by everyone in Wannaska—was five years old when he was indentured to a farmer and given the job of herding geese near a swampy area. He grew to manhood, working for various lengths of time for various farmers. He could visit his family sometimes. He was a small man, barely five feet tall, which was the reason he did not have to serve in the army. He learned to read and

[3] See details of Fyn Island online: http://en.wikipedia.org/wiki/Middelfart

write enough to be confirmed in the Lutheran church in 1866 in Middlefart, Denmark (which means "middle fort").

When he was about nineteen years old, Jens went into a shop in town to get a new pair of wooden shoes. When he came out of the shop, the streets were full of German soldiers in the process of annexing the Schleisswig-Holstein territory between Denmark and Germany. Across the road, a man was shot off the roof he was thatching. Jens thought that act was cruel and unnecessary. He was also angered by the fact the soldiers had to be quartered in the homes of local people. He never forgot and never forgave the actions of these soldiers.

When World War I started, Grandpa Mortensen offered to take care of the farm so that his son Andrew (Ray's father) could enlist in the army and go fight the Germans. Andrew did not want to do that. Later, when Ray was about sixteen years old, he remonstrated with his grandfather about his continued animosity toward Germans. Grandpa moved his pipe to the other side of his mouth, looked off into the distance, and said, "It wasn't your mother or your sisters."

Jens and Ellen Mortensen Emigrate

In 1879 Grandpa signed onto a farm near Grindsted,[4] Denmark. There he met Ellen Marie Jensen. She was born in 1854 in Baggersgaard in Southern Omme County, Veil District, to Jens and Ane Andersen. Her job on this farm was to milk forty cows morning and night. They married and started their family.

Their living conditions were very simple. Though their home was small, food was adequate. Eels were the only source of protein, except at Christmas when the farm owner would butcher the oldest horse and distribute the meat to all the other workers on the farm. One time Ray told Grandpa he didn't think eating eels was especially appetizing, but Grandpa said eels were better than nothing.

A box on their cottage floor served as their bed, with a straw-filled tick for a mattress. Sometimes at night they'd feel movement under the mattress: a bull snake. Grandpa said they felt fortunate to have bull snakes in their home, since that meant there'd be no rats.

---

[4] Grindsted municipality is now abolished. See details at http://en.wikipedia.org/wiki/Grindsted

Grandpa was not happy with the living and social conditions in Denmark at that time, even though Denmark was considered an "enlightened" nation and treated the citizens more fairly and kindly than some other nations. He was especially irritated with the custom that required a person meeting another of a higher rank—a government official, a storekeeper, or a clergyman—to step off the road, remove his hat, and bow until the other person passed. When he lived in America, he never bowed to another person, except maybe in church. Another thing that really angered him was the fact that when Grandma was not milking cows, she was required to pick up chicken droppings from the farm yard and put them into her apron for use on the crop land.

At this time, many people were immigrating to America. Grandpa began to think the only way he could better the living conditions for his family was to leave Denmark. He really wanted to immigrate to New Zealand, but Grandma objected, because the trip to New Zealand was so much longer than the trip to America.

A few years earlier, two of Grandpa's brothers, Morten and Krystan, immigrated to America and settled in Dunlap, Iowa, approximately sixty miles from Sioux City, Iowa. Early in 1889 they sent Grandpa passage money and a promise of employment with an established farmer, so the decision was made for Grandpa to emigrate.

Lutheran Church in Middlefart, Denmark
where Jens and Ellen Mortensen worshipped

Grandpa and Grandma must have had very different feelings about that decision. Grandpa was very eager to take advantage of probably the only opportunity he'd ever get to make a better life for his family. Grandma was probably afraid to be left with four small children, and maybe thought she'd never see her husband again. The plan was for Grandpa to sail to America, and then work hard to save passage for Grandma to follow him to Iowa. Little did he know at the time that when his family joined him in America, there would be a fifth child in his family–Andrew, Ray's father.

So Grandpa sailed to America and worked on a farm in Dunlap, Iowa. Grandpa told Ray that one of the farmers he worked for swore at him a lot of the time. Someone told him how to say "stop" when the man did that. So the next time the man started swearing at him, Grandpa stuck his pitchfork hard into the ground, and said, "Stop," very loudly. That did the trick; the man never swore at him again.

Later that summer Grandpa managed to borrow the money so his family could join him. In October 1889, Grandma said good-bye to her family in Denmark and sailed to America. In those days, the emigrants rarely saw again the family they left behind. There were five children by this time: Annie - age 9, Martha - age 7, Morten - age 5, Christena - age 3, and Andrew, only six weeks old. This was the most difficult time for Grandma, nursing all five children and caring for them on the long journey. Another situation that faced her was the fact she could speak only Danish. During the time aboard ship and until she reached Dunlap, Iowa, she could not converse with anyone else, except one Norwegian sailor who could communicate with her a bit.

Grandma's descendants admired the courage and determination she showed in making this extremely difficult journey. In the Mortensen family history prepared by Ray's sister, Mildred Simmons, she said whenever Grandpa spoke about his trip to America as his "greatest adventure," Grandma would be irate, saying, "Ya, he can talk about adventure. He didn't have five kids with him."

As long and difficult as the journey was, the family was finally reunited in Iowa.

The Jens and Ellen Mortensen Family
Back: Morten, Martha, Annie
Middle: Andrew, Grandpa Jens and Grandma Ellen, Christena
Front: Jens, Marie, Hannah

The following is from papers that Jens and Ellen Mortensen obtained from Danish authorities before their emigration to America. Translation was by Hannah and Marie Mortensen.

> Jens Mortensen, son of that time Bolsmand (or Botsmand) and Kotter weaver, Morten Mortensen and wife, Johanna Marie Jorgensdattter, was born at 'Afjmyds Mans' in Afjmyds County, Northern District the 9 September 1851, eighteen hundred and fifty one, and was baptized November 30 that same year. Which I hereby testify with Afjmyds district church book, according to law.
>
> Confirmed in Middlefart, January 29, 1866
> Mselbye, District Minister

In Omme District Church book shows:
Ellen Marie Jensen, daughter of that time farmer Jens Andersen, and wife, Ane Andersdatter of Baggersgaard, was born in southern Omme County, Veile district, March 20, 'twentieth' 1854 'fifty four' and baptized in S. Omme Church the 25 'twenty-fifth' May same year. Which I hereby testify on behalf of government.

S. Omme Church the 14 October 1889
Ekshyssey, District Minister

Jens and Ellen Mortensen in Iowa

Grandpa Mortensen worked long, hard hours and in time repaid his employer the money advanced for Grandma's fare. The family recalls that Grandpa, though grateful to be able to bring his family to America, didn't respect the farmer who loaned him the money, because he charged Grandpa almost fifty per cent interest. By 1892, Grandpa took out a mortgage for his own land in "Dane Hollow," near Dunlap, Iowa. During the 1890s the family continued to grow. Hannah was born in 1891, Jens in 1894, and then the last, Marie, was born in 1897.

Martha said their mother was afraid of cyclones, which were common in Iowa. If there as a hint of black clouds or if she heard thunder, Grandma gathered all the children and down into the cyclone cellar they'd go. In later years as adults, the family laughed over how they spent so much time down in their cellar in Iowa.

When the boys were partly grown, one of them was up on the roof of the house and later told his brothers he'd seen an empty area in the middle of a neighbor's corn field. Morten became excited. "That's where he's hiding his watermelon field." The patch was soon raided.

One night the boys were coming home after dark, and when they passed the cemetery, they heard strange noises and thought they saw a ghost. They arrived home and told their father what they'd seen and heard. Grandpa got a lamp, and they all retraced their steps—and found a white sow lying in the ditch nursing a brood of piglets.

There was always lots of work to do on the farm: crops of small grains were planted, tended, and harvested. The family prospered; the children went to school, and were confirmed in the Lutheran church. The time spent in school was not very long. Because they were needed to work on the farm, the children went to school only a few months a year. Andrew finished the fourth grade and that was thought to be enough for a farm boy.

School in Dunlap, Iowa
Andrew Mortensen is at far left

About that time, Andrew and a friend of his, Martin Johnson (whose cousin George Johnson later married Andrew's sister Christena), played a naughty trick on the school teacher. As school ended for the summer, the two boys waited until everyone had gone home. When the teacher went out to use the privy, the boys tipped it over so its door faced the ground and then they went home, leaving the teacher trapped inside. It was some time before someone heard the noise the teacher was making and freed her. In later years, when Andrew took his family to Iowa for a visit, he saw Martin and hollered, "Hey, Martin, remember when we tipped over the toilet with the teacher inside?" Martin was embarrassed, because he'd never told anyone about that escapade.

As the young folks reached marriageable age, Grandpa and Grandma had the same problems as a very large number of families. Their young people were attracted to and wanted to marry outside of their parents' ethnic and religious beliefs. I've been told by family members that Grandpa did not bring Danish prejudices to this country. He said he came here to be a good American, and so he was; but religious differences were a new and difficult problem for the family.

Pastor J.A. Jensen's Confirmation Class, Dunlap, Iowa
Andrew Mortensen is at far right
To his left is Martin Johnson, his best friend

Annie, the oldest, married Knudt Lee, a Norwegian from nearby Soldier, Iowa. At least he was a Lutheran, so that was all right, sort of. Martha, though, married Clarence Davis, an American of English descent and another religious affiliation. Martha and her husband moved east and raised their family near Washington, D.C. In time, the dissention lessened.

The Mortensen Family Moves to Roseau County

Knudt Lee's family moved to Wannaska in Roseau County, Minnesota. Named after a local Native American chief, Wannaska was first settled in the mid-1880s by Pete Larson, John Spencer, Martin Grefthen, Matt Johnson, Bernt Thompson, and others.

In 1899 Anton O. Hagen, Knudt Lee's brother-in-law, started a store southwest of Wannaska. In 1900 a post office and store was started by P.O. Fosse and Martin Grefthen. In 1902 A.O. Hagen moved his store onto Knudt's land, and in 1906 Knudt bought out his brother-in-law. Knudt had been appointed postmaster in 1904 and remained so until his death in 1945. Until 1997, the store was owned by Knudt's son, Leland. It has been known as "Lee's Store" since at least 1906, and in

1996 it still contained the post office and was the oldest family-owned business in Roseau County.[5]

By this time Knudt had won the respect and confidence of Grandpa and Grandma, so he was able to convince Grandpa to sell out in Iowa and move to Wannaska. In the cold of February 1906, the family and all their possessions were loaded into a railroad box car and traveled northward to Greenbush, Minnesota, and then overland by wagon to Wannaska.

Grandpa and Grandma purchased the homestead rights from A. Anderson for a farm south of Knudt Lee's farm and store. The next year a house was built, which became the Mortensen farm and home for the next sixty-two years.

Mortensen Farm House outside Wannaska

The style of farming was about the same in Minnesota as it was in Iowa–various small grains and a variety of stock. However, they did not raise corn in northern Minnesota, because the growing season was much shorter than in Iowa.

---

[5] See Lee's Store in *Minnesota Reflection*, from the Roseau County Historical Society online digital archives.

Again, by lots of hard work, the family prospered, gained the respect of neighbors, and entered into activities in the town and vicinity. When the Mortensens moved to Wannaska, they left behind the close ties they had with fellow Danes in Iowa. Here they were the only Danes, surrounded by Norwegians and Swedes.

George Johnson and Christena Mortensen Johnson

Morten Mortensen and Hilda Oslund Mortensen

Perhaps it helps to understand the animosity between the Scandinavian people. For centuries before, at one time or another, Norway, Denmark, or Sweden exercised power over the others and caused them all to hate each other. This dislike came with them when they immigrated to this country and continued almost up to the time of WWII. When Ray was about eight years old, his mother told him that way back in her ancestry was a Swede. Ray cried. The animosity began to lessen as intermarriage occurred, and now it carries on as a source of jokes.

In 1907, George Johnson, a Dane and a Lutheran from Dunlap, Iowa, came up to Wannaska. He stayed awhile and helped Grandpa build his house. He took Christena home to Iowa and married her. They raised their family on their successful farm, growing corn and hogs.

I think George and Christena knew each other before she left Iowa. Orval thinks Grandpa wanted Christena to be married in Iowa in the Danish church there, instead of the Norwegian church in Wannaska.

Andrew Mortensen, January 1914

In 1909 Morten, the oldest son, married Hilda Oslund, a Swedish girl, but a Lutheran. Her father became a bit upset when he heard about slighting references made by a Mortensen concerning Swedes–so much so, he quit going to the same church as the family until Grandpa passed on. But Morten and Hilda prospered and raised their family, and were deeply respected by everyone. Within a few years, the family began to scatter. In 1914, Andrew married Julia Olson, a Norwegian girl, also a Lutheran. The fourth daughter, Hannah, married Chris Hardland, a Norwegian immigrant and a Lutheran, and moved with him to North Dakota in 1916. Jens married Nettie Reed, a girl from the neighboring town of Badger in 1917. In 1919, Marie married Blanchard Hunking.

Blanchard and Nettie were of mixed ethnic origins. Morten and Andrew began their families in and around Wannaska.

Jens Olson Comes from Norway

Jens Olson was born in 1850 in Norway, near a large lake close to Oslo. His father was a shoemaker who moved from farm to farm, making whatever shoes were needed for that farm. Jens told about the feeding arrangements on the farm: the higher the status a person had, the better he ate. As a shoemaker, Jens's father ate with the third rank.

Jens immigrated to North America at the age of seventeen. He was six weeks at sea aboard a sailing ship. For food aboard ship, Jens had a barrel of cooked mush. As mold formed, it was lifted off and the rest eaten. On deck was a water barrel with a cup attached to it. Anyone who needed water had to come to the barrel. If they were ill or couldn't go to the barrel, they didn't get any water.

All things considered, Grandpa Olson thought the trip was a big adventure. He came to North America by way of Canada, eventually coming to live in southern Minnesota, in Fillmore County. A few years later he married Mary Bendicson at Lanesboro. Four children were born to them. In 1878, Minnie came along; then two boys, Carl and Bennie; and in 1891, Julia completed the family. Julia was born in Harmony, Minnesota.

When Julia was about four years old, her mother began to have problems that were treated as mental illness. She was committed to the state hospital for the insane, which was then the only form of treatment. Grandma Olson spent the rest of her life in the mental hospital. It was considered a disgrace for any family to have a member who was "insane." Other family members were tainted with the disease.

At this time Grandpa Olson was a Star Route rural mail carrier, which was a good job for those days. The family thinks that the effect of Grandma being in the hospital not far from where he lived was too much for Grandpa to bear, so he decided to move to another area.

In 1903 Jens and his children moved to Ringbo, Minnesota. Julia worked for her room and board while attending school. She worked for Dr. Penney, whose wife was very helpful, teaching Julia to keep house and to cook.

In 1905 Jens Olson's daughter Minnie and her husband, Abraham Sorter of Holt, Minnesota, persuaded Grandpa Olson to go with them to Roseau County to file for homesteads about three miles east of Wannaska.

Jens Olson family
Top row: Carl Olson, Bennie Olson, Jens Olson
Front row: Julia Olson, Archie Sorter, Minnie Olson Sorter, Abe Sorter

The claims were near each other, but the land was not good, mostly swamp and peat land with some sand ridges. There was, however, heavy timber around them. Abe ran a small steam-powered saw mill, did some blacksmithing, and was also a carpenter, a sort of jack-of-all-trades. Two sons came along, Archie and Lloyd. Later they moved to a smaller, drier place closer to Wannaska.

Grandpa Olson, Carl, Bennie, and Julia made their home in a small log cabin in the woods. Bennie kept the family in good supply of meat. Deer were scarce in that area at that time, so the game he shot for the family was usually moose, which with potatoes and other garden items was their meager diet. Moose was not the best tasting of game animals, but it was plentiful.

ꕥ

Money was scarce, so the Olson men went to North Dakota to work the harvest. This money bought their flour, sugar, and tobacco supplies. When the men were working the harvests in the Dakotas, Julia (about fourteen years old) was left behind alone, quite far from the neighbors and very frightened—especially when her father's friends came around looking for him. She wouldn't answer when they knocked at the door, and remained very quiet until they finally left. Sometimes these men had been drinking a bit, but these men were just lonely old bachelors looking for their friend Jens Olson. The family still anguishes for her, thinking of how frightened she must have been during these times.

Jens Olson was a large man who had a good sense of humor. He'd slap his thigh and laugh long and loudly. Ray said Orval was about the same size as his grandfather, with a hearty laugh like his, also.

Jens marveled at new modes of travel. In the early 1920s, someone took him for a ride in their new automobile, which had curtains on the sides, with Eisenglass windows (mica in thin sheets, which functions like clear plastic). He just couldn't get over how much nicer it was to ride in something as modern as that. Grandpa Olson rubbed his hands over the sides of the windows, saying, "My, isn't this nice." He thought things just couldn't get any better.

Jens Olson followed the true Viking tradition as to hospitality. We might think of the ancient Vikings as fierce pillagers, killers, rapists, and robbers—and that they were, to all other people but their own. But they had strict rules of conduct amongst themselves. According to some of the ancient sagas, travelers or visitors must receive a full welcome and the best a host could offer—for three days; after that time, a visitor should travel on.

Jens Olson was also a devout Christian. He followed the teachings of Jesus and shared what he had with those in need. So he found it difficult to deny hospitality, no matter how meager it was, to those who came to his door. I'm sure he said, "*Velcommen til vart hjen* (welcome to my home). Come in, sit down, have a cup of coffee."

A picture found in every Bible book store shows an elderly bearded man, his head bowed in prayer, saying Grace and ready to eat a meager meal, with his Bible close by. All members of Ray's family have a copy of this picture in their homes, because they say it shows how their Grandfather Olson looked and lived.

When his friends were lonesome or hungry or needed a place to stay awhile, they'd say, "Let's go see good old Jens Olson." Julia was bothered by this, because their food supplies were scarce and their cabin small. She felt these men took advantage of her father. He'd tell her that maybe some were taking advantage of him, so she should decide who to turn away. Julia couldn't do that, so the visitors–whom some called bums–still came to see "Good old Jens Olson."

Julia Olson circa 1912

As a young person, Julia didn't understand her father's feelings about welcoming his visitors, but when she was established in her own home, she served many a visitor. Later, when she could no longer stay in her home and had to go to a nursing home, her worst disappointment was that she could no longer serve us a cup of coffee.

"Good old Jens Olson" had more than his share of tragedy in life. First, what happened to his wife; then, not long after making his home near Wannaska, his son Carl was kicked in the head by a horse. Carl survived the kick, but it left him unable to control his anger, and he had to be committed to the state hospital for the insane. A few years later, Jens's remaining son, Bennie, died of cholera. In 1928, Jens Olson lost his son-in-law and a grandson to influenza.

ฐ

Andrew and Julia Mortensen, June 1914

In about 1912, Julia worked for Annie Mortensen Lee, who was a very good cook and housekeeper. Julia was a good student. When she worked for Annie, she met Annie's brothers, Jens and Andrew. In 1914, Julia and Andrew were married in Andrew's parents' house on the farm, which would be their home for fifty-four years.

Later, Jens Olson's shack was moved onto the Mortensen farm, and he lived there for some time. Grandpa Olson died in 1939, after two years being bed-ridden. He was unable to care for himself, and Julia did all she could to make him comfortable. He'd sleep during the day and spend the nights talking and singing to himself. He was a very large man, and Julia had a difficult time caring for him. But Julia, being Julia, never once complained.

At Grandpa Olson's funeral, an old-timer told Ray, "Jens Olson never had a dime, but he never had an enemy, either."

Jens and Ellen Mortensen in Wannaska

After Ray was born in 1915, Grandpa Mortensen rented his farm to Andrew. Then he and Grandma purchased a small plot of land in town on the bank of the Roseau River. They had a small house, a cow, some chickens, and room for a large garden. They lived there until Grandma passed away in 1941. They were very happy living in their own place. Grandpa continued helping Andrew at the farm as much as he was needed. They were always involved in anything happening around the area. Many years later, when Andrew's daughter Mildred married Russell Simmons, they lived in Grandpa's house in Wannaska.

A few years after moving into town, Grandpa was waiting for his mail at Lee's Store. A group of folks were discussing a problem: they'd purchased a dish cabinet for a newly married couple and shivareed them the evening before, but the couple wouldn't invite the celebrants into the house for refreshments, which when the present was to be given to the couple. So, what to do with the cabinet? Grandpa, laughing, said, "You can shivaree me any time." Even though Grandpa and Grandma had been married over fifty years, that evening they were shivareed. They treated the group and received the gift.

For those who don't understand the custom of a shivaree: After dark when the newlyweds retire for the night, a group of neighbors and friends gather outside the home and make lots of noise, sometimes involving gun shots in the air or even setting off dynamite. The newlyweds are supposed to invite the crowd inside and serve them refreshments. After a time spent celebrating, the crowd presents a gift to the young folks, and they all go home, leaving the newlyweds in peace. The custom showed acceptance of the couple into the community. With most couples, the feeling was that if they weren't shivareed, the local neighbors didn't like them.

Grandpa and Grandma Mortensen attended every gathering in town: church, barn dances, vaudeville or lantern shows, programs at the school, and anything else that happened in the area. Grandma could not speak English, but was always at Grandpa's side. They were very well liked by everyone around, and they were always referred to as "Grandpa" and "Grandma" by everyone.

༄

Once a week, Grandma walked from Wannaska to the farm to visit with Julia and the grandchildren. She always stopped at Lee's Store and bought a small bag of candy for the children. They'd see her coming down the road and eagerly anticipate the offer of the candy they knew she'd bring. The children were taught not to ask, but to wait for the candy to be offered. Sometimes Grandma and Julia would get to talking, and Grandma would forget about her bag of candy. Ray remembered their mouths watering in anticipation.

Mentioning "Grandma and Julia talking" needs some explanation. Grandma spoke Danish and Julia spoke Norwegian, but somehow they had good visits with each other. One year Grandma's daughters decided Grandma Mortensen needed time for herself. Grandpa was good to her, but the girls thought he expected her to wait on him too much. The girls suggested that Grandpa take a trip to Iowa, to visit the family there. Grandpa went alone, because Grandma did not enjoy traveling. He was gone for two weeks.

Grandma cried every day while Grandpa was gone, because she was so lonesome for him. She said, "What is that old fool doing anyway, staying so long? I want him to come home where he belongs."

Grandma couldn't talk easily with her grandchildren, because none of them learned Danish. Ray thought Grandpa teased Grandma about learning to speak English, so she quit trying. In his older years, Ray was sad that Grandma missed talking with her grandchildren, since he loved talking to his own grandchildren.

When her other work was done, Grandma would spin and knit wool that she'd washed and carded. Each Christmas, each grandchild received socks, mittens, and a scarf knitted by Grandma. Grandma gave Mildred her spinning wheel, which she treasured greatly.

ℵ

Many humorous stories were told about Grandpa; many he told himself. One time, Grandpa Mortensen and a few young men were walking from the farm towards Wannaska. Grandpa, in the rear, overheard someone say they'd better not walk too fast for the old man. Well, Grandpa decided to show these young folks he wasn't as old as they thought, so he began to walk faster. He soon walked right on passed them and kept it up all the way to Wannaska, grinning all the way.

As an example of Grandpa Mortensen's many stories, he told Ray about a wake held for a neighbor back in Denmark. The dead man's friends partied for about three days. They had a great time, and then everyone went home—but had to be called back, because it seems they forgot to bury the dead man.

Before automobiles, men were always trying to find a better horse, so a lot of trading occurred. Every Saturday was horse-trading day in Roseau, eagerly anticipated by anyone wanting to trade his horse. One time, Grandpa traded horses three times and came home $30 to the good. Even the most Christian person did not think it was wrong to stretch the good points of his horse, or the bad points would not be mentioned if possible.

Grandpa Mortensen, as upright and honorable man as he was, was a very sharp horse-trader. One time he traded the horse that he used with the buggy to go to church. He thought he got the best of the deal, but he didn't know that the new mare was a "swisher." This meant that while trotting along, she'd urinate and at the same time switch her tail around, splashing the moisture over whoever was riding in the buggy. This habit was discovered while driving the horse home.

Well, Grandpa had to get rid of that horse as soon as possible. His pride wouldn't allow him to let the person from whom he'd received the horse know that Grandpa had been taken in the deal. So when the first trader asked Grandpa how he liked the new mare, Grandpa said the horse was just fine. But he soon traded that horse to another person without revealing the horse's bad habit. Ray said his own father was almost as slick a horse-trader as Grandpa.

3: Early Days in Wannaska

Picnic at Wannaska circa 1912
Front left: Andrew Mortensen; Fourth from left: Hannah Mortensen

The Old-Timers Describe Early Life

Among the earliest settlers in Wannaska were John Spencer and Pete Larsen, who later donated the land for the Riverside Lutheran Church. The first school in Wannaska was held at the John Spencer homestead. Other early settlers were Martin Grefthen, Matt Johnson, and Bernt Thompson. Martin and P.O. Fosse started the first store and post office in 1900, and continued until Knudt Lee took over the store and post office in 1906.

Pete Larsen, who lived alone in a shack on the upper reaches of the Roseau River, was asked once if he'd ever been lost in the woods. He said, "No, not really lost, just turned around a few times." Once, he said, he shot and wounded a deer. He tracked it through the snow for about three days. He came to a small river with a cabin on the other side. He crossed over the river and entered the cabin (this was permissible in the woods, when necessary). After making a fire and beginning to eat, he realized he was in his own cabin. He claimed that he had not crossed any other river during his time trailing the deer, so he figured he had gone around the headwaters of the branch of the Roseau River where he lived.

Pete told another story: while a little ways from his cabin, he wounded a bear, which began to charge him. He ran toward his cabin, reloading his gun as he ran. When he got to the doorway, he turned and shot the bear again. The bear kept coming at him until it died in Pete's doorway. He didn't want to have any close encounters with bears after that experience.

Another old-timer told about how he and his wife spent their first winter on their homestead, seeing no other human beings all winter, living in their cabin by a lake. They had to turn loose their animal (I don't remember if it was a horse or a cow) to fend for itself, because there was no hay for its food. They found it the next spring, quite undernourished but still alive. The couple had nothing to eat all that winter except the fish they caught in the lake. They didn't even have salt for their fish. When asked if the situation was difficult to endure, they said, "No, we weren't bored. We hadn't been married very long before then."

Native Americans of the Wannaska Area

Bernt Thompson spent the first winter in Wannaska living in a cave dug out of the river bank. He told Ray how friendly the Native Americans were. When no strangers were around, they'd laugh and joke with each other, but when a stranger appeared, they became silent and straight-faced.

When more European settlers came to northern Minnesota, they found the local Chippewa tribe to be friendly. One of the local Native Americans said in the olden days that no one stole from anyone. You could leave belongings any place and no one would take it.

One of the most admired Native American was Mickinock.[6] He lived near Wannaska and Roseau, and had a great influence upon the tribes around there. When any local tribe members drank too much

[6] See Mickinock and his daughters in *Minnesota Reflections*, from the Roseau County Historical Society digital archives at http://reflections.mndigital.org/cdm/singleitem/collection/ros/id/239

liquor, Mickinock warned the settlers to stay inside their cabins until they sobered up, and he kept telling his tribe members to leave the settlers alone.

In 1901 the homesteaders became alarmed by a rumor that the Native Americans were going to rebel. They heard the Native Americans were buying a lot of guns and ammunition. So the settlers loaded their families into their wagons and took off a ways to the south. They stayed a couple of weeks, and when no news of any disturbance reached them, they sent a couple of fellows back to learn what had happened.

The two scouts discovered that Mickinock had been going from farm to farm, feeding and watering all the settlers' stock. It was said Mickinock asked those left behind around Roseau to go tell the missing settlers to come back home. He said, "I can't feed these animals all winter."

Mickinock's wife's hair was a different color from the rest of the local Native Americans, brown instead of black. Mickinock explained it as proof of a legend the Native Americans told concerning a shipwreck on Roseau Lake a very long time before, involving seven men, two women, and five children. They all had blond hair and blue eyes. The adults died the next year, but the children survived to adulthood and married Native American; hence, the hair color differences among the natives.

This might be related to the Kensington Rune Stone in southern Minnesota, which tells of a group of Vikings entering what must have been Hudson Bay and traveling down the river systems to where they left a record of their troubles with the "Skralings," the Viking word for North American natives. No one knows whatever became of these travelers. The authenticity of the Kensington Rune Stone is questioned.[7]

Native Americans that lived in and around Roseau were well liked and told lots of stories of the old times. One was named Kaukaugeesik. He was a medicine man who was born on the banks of the Lake of the Woods, near Warroad. He said he didn't know how old he was, because his people did not keep records in that way, but based on his earliest remembrances, he was well over one hundred years old.

My brother-in-law, Russell Summons, told a story about Kaukaugeesik. As a young boy, Russell's father was bringing a pail of buttermilk from a neighbor's farm and was met on the road by Kaukaugeesik, who

---

[7] See Kensington Rune Stone at http://en.wikipedia.org/wiki/Kensington_Runestone

asked him for a drink from the pail. Kaukaugeesik took a big drink, thinking it was fresh milk, but when he discovered it was buttermilk, he spat it out explosively. This frightened the boy, who took off running toward his home, with Kaukaugeesik running after him. The boy thought the man intended to harm him, but all Kaukaugeesik wanted was give back the pail of buttermilk.

When Kaukaugeesik died in 1968, his funeral was held in the Warroad High School gymnasium, with a native ceremony.

One of the first homesteaders in the area told about a local Native American custom. The homestead family might be sitting at the supper table when one or two Native Americans came in, sat down, ate, and then left without saying a word to anyone. A day or two later, a duck or a couple of fish or maybe some venison would be left on the door step.

Most Native Americans gradually moved to live near Warroad, though some lived on a reservation east of Roseau.

In the early 1930s, a group of Native Americans camped in their wigwams east of Wannaska. While the men hunted rabbits, the women dug camas roots. The rabbits were sun-dried and smoked. The Native Americans had horses to trade. The men would arrange a trade, but couldn't close it until their wives checked the horse all over and said it was OK.

"If You Can't Find It at Lee's Store..."

Lee's Store was the hub of the community in Wannaska. Knudt's family lived in an addition built onto the west and north side of the store. People gathered at the store, getting their wives' grocery lists filled and waiting for the mail to get in.

In the early days, the mail was hauled in a horse-drawn wagon. The carrier left Wannaska at 6:00 a.m. The mail got to Roseau by train, and the driver arrived back in Wannaska at any time from 7:00 p.m. to 10:00 p.m. The time the mail arrived depended on the weather, since the roads were not reliable. In winter, the snow was deep, so a sleigh was used. In the rainy seasons, the roads were full of potholes and the mud very sticky.

Waiting for the mail was a great time for neighbors to visit around the big stove, swapping outlandish stories with straight faces, in the

Scandinavian manner of telling extremely tall stories as if their lives depended upon them being believed.

At Lee's Store, ~1906

Knudt Lee, third from left; Annie Lee, third from right

Knudt Lee gave credit to most of his customers. Often he waited a long time to be paid. When his customers received their cream checks, they most often cashed them at Lee's Store and paid their bills at that time. When Knudt Lee died in 1945, he had a lot of unpaid credit slips in his papers.

Lee's Store was typical of general stores that operated in other small towns. It was said, "If Knudt doesn't have it, you don't need it." The post office was in one corner. The store contained most everything needed on the farm or in the home, tools of all sorts, and of course, groceries. The meat sold was not cut and displayed like in the stores today. If a side of beef was in the cooler and you wanted some, Knudt would slice up whatever cut was next on the carcass.

What made Lee's Store different from others was Knudt. Everyone knew Knudt would deal with them better than anyone else. He was extremely honest and well-liked by everyone with whom he dealt. He was involved in numerous activities in the area. He ran a farm besides operating the store and bought cattle, sheep, wool, and eggs. The grown sheep and cattle were herded to Roseau and loaded into cattle cars at the Great Northern Railroad. Sometimes Knudt traveled with the cattle to Minneapolis and on to Chicago to sell them.

One time a customer telephoned Knudt and asked him to come to his farm to look over some cattle he wanted Knudt to buy. When Knudt got to the farm, he discovered a gathering of friends having a party—and no cattle to buy. Later when this was discussed in the store, someone commented how angry Knudt was to be tricked that way.

Another fellow replied, "Vell, I don't know about dat. I noticed he didn't come home for tree days."

A cat—I think it belonged to Annie, Knudt's wife (and Andrew Mortensen's sister)—kept getting into mischief in the store, so Knudt kept chasing it out. One time it became extremely annoying, so Knudt grabbed it and wiped its rear end with a kerosene rag. The cat let out a terrific yowl and went flying out of the store. It stayed away for several days, and never again came close to Knudt.

Knudt was always in a hurry and sometimes spoke without thinking what he was saying. One time he told a customer in the store he had a special on for canned sardines. He said, "I'll sell them to you for five cents a can, or three for a quarter." It took time for Knudt to understand why all the men in the store were laughing so hard.

When Knudt went fishing with a group to the Lake of the Woods once, they camped for a couple of days, having a very good time. On their last day of fishing, a fish bit on Knudt's line, and he got so excited, he began reeling in his line. That didn't go fast enough for him, so he tossed his pole in the water and began to pull his line in by hand, to the great amusement of the others in the party.

Over the years Knudt hired quite a number of helpers in the store. Two teen-aged boys, Bedford Grefthen and Morriel Mortensen (a cousin of Ray's) worked there quite often.

Once a traveling evangelist, in town for a series of services, came into the store when these two boys were working. He wanted to buy a collar for his shirt—an old-fashioned detachable, stiff collar that fastened under a person's chin with a small metal button. The boys knew exactly what the man wanted, but they pretended they thought he wanted a horse collar (used to hook up horses for driving). They brought out for him to see every size and style of horse collar in the store and went to extremes trying to sell them to the man. The evangelist was so exasperated by what he perceived to be their ignorance, he mentioned the trouble at the store in his sermon that night. The boys, however, thought they never had so much fun in their lives.

Another time when these two were in charge of the store, business was slow, so Bedford and Morriel decided to cut each other's hair. Each wanted his hair cut short–so short they eventually shaved each other's heads; but one said that wasn't enough, so he shaved his eyebrows, too. Ray and Orval said the result was hard to describe, it was so bizarre.

One day a dog came into Lee's Store with a set of false teeth in his mouth. Ole, waiting for his mail, said, "Oh, dere dey are. I lost dem last night." He wiped them off on his shirt and popped them back into his mouth.

Other Businesses in Wannaska

A steam-powered flour mill operated in Wannaska from 1903 to 1907. The Wannaska Creamery Association was organized in 1907. Later it was associated with the Land O'Lakes Creamery organization. Jens Mortensen was the butter maker there for a while before he moved with his family to Aurora, Oregon in 1923.

In 1907 the first restaurant opened in town with rooms to rent upstairs. The Farmers State Bank operated from 1915 until 1926, when it was bought out by Citizens State Bank of Roseau.

Since those days, a few more businesses began operating in Wannaska; another grocery store operated during the Fifties and Sixties; a service station and garage are there now. Wannaska is still a small town.

ꝏ

During the 1930s and 1940s a man in town did an assortment of jobs, working as a general handyman. He could barely read and write, but was practically a genius of another kind. He could fix just about anything, tinker with car engines, and make hard-to-get parts. With no concept of how much his work was worth, he never charged enough. For a while, until he was caught, he made his own license plates. One time he and his brother stole money from Knudt Lee, were caught, and served time in prison. When his time was up, he came back to town, but he never again took anything that didn't belong to him.

Stories from the Wannaska Old Timers

One neighbor became the extremely proud father of twins. Friends came to see the family. While sitting around the table drinking coffee, he remarked proudly, "I think it is every woman's ambition to have twins."

His wife had not been getting much rest since the babies were born; one or the other seemed to cry most of the time. When she heard her husband make this remark, she wearily said, "That's what you think."

ꟈ

Goats made another neighbor's life interesting for a while. The goats got inside the house and found the family's supply of canned food—not home canned, but store-bought canned food with paper labels. The goats ate all the labels off the cans. As a result, the family never knew what they were having for supper until the cans were opened.

The goats also gave their owner trouble by not staying inside the fenced pasture. No sooner were they rounded up and replaced inside the fence than out they'd go again. The farmer discovered that when the fence was erected, the angle braces at the corners were on the inside of the fence, so the goats just walked up an angled brace and jumped out.

ꟈ

A family from Holland, the DeBrouffs, became neighbors of Aunt Minnie and Lloyd Sorter, Ray's aunt and cousin. The family consisted of four brothers and one sister. Upon their arrival in New York City, they went to a restaurant. They couldn't speak or read English, so they pointed to an item listed on the menu. When their meal was served, they discovered they had ordered oysters, which they'd never seen before. Even though they were hungry, they weren't hungry enough to eat them.

ꟈ

Two brothers worked and lived in Detroit. The other brothers and sister came to Wannaska to live. Wannaska was chosen haphazardly by sticking a pin in a map of Minnesota. They were hard working people who were very friendly when visitors came, but they did not go visit others much. Ray's mother felt sorry for the sister, who kept house for her brothers but had no close friends.

Eventually the two brothers and the sister came to Oregon to live a few miles southeast of Salem. They lived there a few years and then returned to Wannaska. One brother married, but he had no children.

ꟈ

A family of boys, the Palms, created quite a bit of excitement several times. Once they played "William Tell" by shooting things off each other's head with their .22 rifle. I don't think Ray's mother ever knew that happened.

The Palm boys liked to climb up to the top of a tree and jump over to another tree. Most made it, but one didn't. He lived, but was paralyzed from the waist down. Later, he learned to repair watches. All the local people brought him their watches to be fixed.

ꟈ

Fred Johnson was a very tall man and his wife was rather short. When they came to Roseau to shop, Fred would visit a tavern to partake of a few beers and visit with friends. When his wife finished her shopping, she'd suggest to Fred it was time to go home.

He'd answer, "Ya, Mama, after a little while."

When she thought the "little while" got to be too long, she'd lose her patience and march into the tavern, stretch her arm up high and grab Fred by his ear to lead him out.

All the while he'd be saying, "Ya, ya, Mama, I'm coming, I'm coming."

ꟈ

A homesteading couple lived a ways out of town in a wooded area; the wife was confined to a wheelchair. One day the husband had to go to town and left his wife at home. While he was gone, a tornado came through and lifted the house from around his wife. When he returned, he discovered her sitting in her chair by the stove, but everything else was gone. His wife was not injured, but there was a lot of talk for a long time by friends, concerned about how frightened she must have been.

ꟈ

Rafe Olson had quite an evening once. After he had a bit too much to drink with his friends, he passed out. His friends put him on a toboggan to take him home, but they didn't notice his head was hanging over the edge of the toboggan, banging on the snowy road all the way home. Afterwards, he had quite a headache, but other than that, he was all right. He was a hard-headed Norwegian.

ꟈ

One incident in Wannaska was a source of amusement for many people, but not Mrs. Garrison. She was quite a large woman and one day she fell backwards into her washtub and couldn't get up. It took quite a time for anyone to help her, because everyone was laughing so much. She didn't think it funny, though she usually had a fine sense of humor.

ꟗ

In the early 1920s and 1930s, a large number of homesteaders still lived out in the jack-pine backwoods. These bachelors lived alone in their small shacks, just barely getting by. Many more men than women lived in the county then. Some were lonely enough to advertise in magazine "Lonely Hearts" columns and began to correspond with women who were looking for husbands. Sometimes a bachelor would find a woman who'd come to meet him, and they'd be married. A few of these mail-order brides came to the Wannaska area and got along pretty well with the men they married. I think they were better off than where they'd been living. Other bachelors never married, but lived out their lives alone in the backwoods.

ꟗ

Coffee was an important stable in the diet of the old-time homesteaders and also with the later farmers. Since money was so very scarce, the supply of coffee had to be stretched. A coffee pot was quite large—maybe 12 cups. This stayed on the back of the stove after the first boiling, with water and coffee grounds added as needed each day, until the grounds filled a good part of the pot. Water was then added to be boiled one last time, "to get the good out of it." Then the grounds were turned out onto a flat baking pan, placed in the oven to dry, and then mixed with tobacco and chewed for their "snuff."

Though others saw this as real economy, the Mortensens and the Olsons did not follow this custom.

ꟗ

Some boys playing in the woods south of the school discovered some brand-new equipment for a still. Knowing what it was, they took it apart to examine it. They left it all where they found it, but the men who had intended to use the equipment never built the still. Since it had been disturbed, they thought the Revenue officers had found it and would arrest them if they did anything with the equipment.

ꟗ

A fellow named Bill Smallrider lived some distance east of the Mortensen farm. When he drove his horse and wagon home from town, he'd be hollering or shouting to himself as he passed the farm. He was heard coming long before he could be seen. He had a long beard and frightened Ray's sister Lois. Someone told her he was Santa Claus, which she believed for a long time.

ꝏ

Pete Olson came to visit the Mortensen farm occasionally, always with a few dogs along in his wagon. The dogs scattered around the yard, but when Pete was ready to leave, he'd give a whistle and say, "Come on," and they'd all jump back into the wagon. Pete had such a way with dogs or horses that within a few minutes with him, any of the animals would go home with him.

ꝏ

Before automobiles were common, peddlers visited farms. The first peddlers in the old days carried large packs on their backs containing a variety of items such as needles, thread, scissors, small pots, and other such things. Gradually the peddlers began to drive horse-pulled wagons that could carry a much larger variety of household goods.

The Watkins man—not always the same man, of course—sold cooking items, baking powder, soda, spices, and flavoring extracts. Julia thought that Watkins vanilla was the best brand. He also had a variety of pudding mixes. Julia and the rest of the Mortensen family liked the lemon pudding the best. The Watkins man also carried liniment for sore muscles and a mixture for stomach ache that was blackberry flavored. Grandpa Mortensen liked that medicine when it was needed.

The Watkins man also came to homes in Portland where I grew up. In those days, housewives did not drive to the store whenever they ran out of vanilla or other small items, so these peddlers served a good purpose.

ꝏ

Carl and Tina Nelson were the Mortensens' close neighbors and friends. Carl had a variety of talents: he made violins and played them, made false teeth, and learned taxidermy.

Tina was a good lefse maker who could roll it very thin. Tina made a lot of lefse. She'd take it to the grocery store in Wannaska to be sold, and took lefse orders from people. The money she made came in handy, because times were hard for the Nelsons.

In 1977 Ray and I visited Wannaska with two of our children. We went to Carl's home to see him. By this time Tina had been dead for several years and Carl was alone. He was almost 90 years old. His clothes were a bit disheveled and his hat had holes in it, out of which sprigs of his hair protruded, and he wasn't wearing his false teeth. Ray asked Carl how his brother Alfred was doing, who was in a nursing home. Carl said, "Not too bad, but he isn't in as good shape as I am."

ꝏ

Carl Nelson had quite a hard time learning to drive a car. Some friends had gathered at Carl's home, discussing cars. Carl got his Model T started and began to drive around and around the house. He was doing fine, but when he wanted to stop the car, he couldn't remember how to do that. As Carl approached his friends, he shouted, "How do I stop this thing?"

They yelled back what to do, but by then Carl had driven past and couldn't hear what they said. This went on for several trips around the house. Finally, Carl slowed the car down so he could nudge his house. That worked, but the nudge had enough force to jar the house; all the dishes fell out of the cupboard, upsetting Tina, Carl's wife.

Other old-timers had similar problems learning to drive. It wasn't an easy transition from driving horses or oxen ahead of wagons, buggies, or plows to operating an inanimate machine. One fellow was driving to Wannaska from Roseau and thought he was driving too fast. He forgot how to slow down by using the brakes, so he grabbed the steering wheel with both hands, shoved a foot on the dashboard, and began to yell, "Whoa! Whoa!"

With the arrival of automobiles, roads had to be drastically improved, because potholes and muddy roads slowed the cars and trucks. Gradually the main roads were graveled, and after WWII, they were black-topped.

ꝏ

During the long, cold winters of northern Minnesota, traveling far from home was difficult. For entertainment before radio and TV became common, neighbors gathered in each other's homes to play cards, usually whist or sometimes penny-ante poker (with matches used instead of poker chips).

One winter Elling Williamson and Carl and Alfred Nelson decided to have bit of fun with another neighbor, Ed Anderson. Ed often was teased in one way or another, but he did not always understand he was being teased, which added to the fun for the teasers. Elling and the Nelson brothers went to quite a bit of preparation for this escapade. First, they killed a rabbit, drained and kept the blood, cleaned the intestines, and filled them with the blood. They wrapped the blood-filled intestines around Elling's head and placed his hat on his head. Then they took a shotgun shell apart, filled the shell again with just the powder, and reloaded the gun, which was placed near the table.

After these preparations, Elling called Ed Anderson on the telephone to ask him to come over and play cards. Ed came and they all began to play. All of a sudden, Carl and Elling pretended to get mad at each other; Carl grabbed the shotgun and fired at Elling, who grabbed his head. This caused the rabbit's blood to gush all over Elling. He fell to the floor, pretending to be dead.

Without a word, Ed went outside, put on his skis and went home.

The next morning, Carl called Ed on the phone again and said they had to bury Elling and would he, Ed, come over and help? Ed agreed to that and came to the house again. He was very surprised to see Elling sitting at the table, drinking coffee.

Ray never said what Ed's reaction was to all of this. He always told the story to demonstrate the Scandinavian custom of not getting involved with other people's business.

☙

Elling Williamson was liked by everyone. He had a large family, was a part-time farmer, a woodcutter (sometimes at odd hours), and did any other jobs to earn money. He was also liked by all the kids in the area. Elling talked with them, not down to them. He was a great storyteller and could hold an audience until late in the evening when visiting.

When friends like the Williamsons visited and stories began to be exchanged, the time passed, and soon Ray and his brothers had to go to bed—not at all eagerly. Later their mother would find the boys on the floor of their bedroom, sound asleep with their ears near the floor grate.

One time several fellows sat around Elling's kitchen table drinking coffee, like good Scandinavians do, and Elling bragged about what a good marksman he was.

He said, "I could shoot the eye out of that rooster across the yard." And he did.

His wife became very angry. She said, "I just traded for that new rooster." She fixed chicken for supper that night, but not happily. Farm wives took charge of their chickens, and every other year or so traded each other's roosters to keep their chickens from getting too inbred.

ꝏ

In and around Roseau, everyone's best friend was Dr. John Delmore, who arrived in Roseau in 1909 to begin his practice. He had recently married and decided to go to Roseau. He was warmly welcomed and for many years was the only doctor in that area. Later on, in 1930, his son, Dr. Jack as he was always called, became his partner. In 1943, another son, Robert, became a doctor, also.

Dr. Delmore was a most dedicated doctor. He had a large practice in Roseau and would travel long ways out of town to treat house-bound patients. During the flu epidemic in 1918, about the only sleep he got was while letting his horse find its way to the next farm. Since money was scarce in those days, he was paid with farm produce.

For years, with midwife Mrs. Oslund, he delivered most of the babies in the area. When the local folks saw Mrs. Oslund riding by with some farmer, they knew there'd soon be a new baby nearby.

Sometimes Dr. Delmore seemed a bit gruff when talking to his patients. A woman rushed into his office, exclaiming, "Doctor, doctor, my baby swallowed a nickel. What should I do?" Without taking his attention away from the person he had been examining, Dr. Delmore answered, "Don't worry. You'll get your nickel back," and kept on with his patient.

Maybe Dr. Delmore didn't have a smooth bedside manner, but he was so busy taking care of so many people, they all knew they could trust him with their illnesses. His dream of a local hospital and clinic was a long time coming true. But after WWII, it was fulfilled with a very good medical facility in Roseau.

Not all the families in the area went to the doctor when ill. They used odd substances to treat family members for various illnesses. One father gave sugar with turpentine in a spoon for stomach ache. His son told Ray he had to be very, very sick before he'd tell his dad after a dose like that. One young girl came down with appendicitis, but the doctor was not called. The girl died and was placed in a homemade coffin without being embalmed. At the funeral, the coffin was opened. The girl's hair hadn't been combed, and because the weather was very hot, the odor was unbearable. Ray said it was the worst funeral ever.

ɛɔ

In later years, when we lived in Hubbard, a bachelor moved into a house down the road from us. After visiting a few times with the new neighbor, Ray mentioned that he'd lived near the Lake of the Woods. Our neighbor said he used to vacation in Warroad to fish. He said he'd spend some evenings in the local tavern, where a group of Norwegians sat around a big table, drinking beer, and telling tall stories.

Our friend said he listened to these fellows tell the biggest lies he'd ever heard. They all knew each was lying, but they spent the evening without cracking so much as a smile, acting as if they believed every story told. It was just a Scandinavian way of passing an evening, to our neighbor's great amusement.

ɛɔ

Ray easily slipped into the vernacular of the northern Minnesota Scandinavian dialect (which should be considered a separate language) when he told these stories. A goodly number of people living in northern Minnesota talked as if they were "just off the boat"—sounding like new immigrants.

Here are some of the phrases Ray used (spelled phonetically):

Pasta du yenta – Be careful, little girl.

Pasta du poicka – Be careful, little boy.

Manga takk – Many thanks; said after a meal to thank the cook.

Tussen takk – Thousand thanks.

Isha da – Usually describing something messy.

Fie da – Something disgusting or shameful.

Uff da – Usually accompanied by a deep sigh and meaning many different things: after a large meal, lifting something heavy, being very tired, or anything else you want it to mean.

When Ray talked in the Minnesota dialect, he was always in a happy mood. A day before he passed away, he began his Minnesota talk with his daughters Christine and Sally. We were all smiling as he talked and sang a song or two he liked:

> Ole Olson, ya dey all call me "Ole,"
> I don't know how dey found out my name.
> I never told any dem fellers,
> But it's "Ole" yust da same

ཕ

4: Wannaska School, Church, and Social Life

Riverside Church construction and roofing

Wannaska School Days

The first school in Wannaska was held in 1902 at the John Spencer homestead in Grimstad Township. The next year a school house was built in Wannaska at the cost of $350. Until 1946, grades one through eight were taught in that one room. Then seven other neighboring school houses were moved to the school yard in Wannaska, and students were bused in from the other towns. Then a lunchroom was built. Eventually a new school was built to house all students in the district.

Often students from immigrant families didn't speak English when they started school, but before long, they could speak English and were teaching their parents at home to speak English. Most immigrants were eager to become Americans and to speak English. Sometimes their grammar lacked refinement, but their pride was strong. One time when an old timer's loyalty was questioned, he replied haughtily, "I'm yust as good American as nobody."

Teachers boarded with different families in the community during the school year. They were expected to keep the schoolroom clean, and in winter to get to school early enough to start the fire in the big stove. Children brought their lunches in different containers. Ray took his lunch in a lard pail. His favorite sandwich was rolled up left-over pancakes, usually spread with brown sugar.

The teachers were expected to maintain order in the classroom, and most students understood that if they got in trouble at school, they'd be in trouble at home, too. But sometimes mischief happened. One time a boy pinned the end of a ball of string onto the back pocket of Ray's cousin, Lloyd Sorter, who often was in trouble. Lloyd knew the string was pinned to his pocket, and he walked carefully all around the room, pretending he was looking for something, all the time leaving more of the ball of string trailing behind. The giggling of the rest of the class alerted the teacher to what was happening, She made Lloyd rewind the string–which did not hurt Lloyd's feelings or dampen his delight.

Wannaska School, June 19, 1919
Back, third from right (in straw hat): Archie Sorter
Front, third from right: Elmer Mortensen
End on right: Morriel Mortensen

One boy in school was always getting others in trouble by tattling to the teacher. Once when Lloyd misbehaved, he was tattled on and had to stay after school. Lloyd's friends waylaid the tattler, held him down until Lloyd was released from school and caught up with them. The resulting fight settled things, for a while.

When Lloyd was young, he was in a lot of trouble at school and in a lot of fights. The older members of the family were sure he'd continue to be in trouble when he was grown. How mistaken they all were.

One day the reading lesson was about how sugar cane was grown and refined. A boy was asked to describe the process, but he hadn't read the lesson, so he couldn't answer. The teacher then asked a girl the same question, which she answered. As the boy listened, his eyes widened in surprise, and he said, "Oh, I thought it grew in lumps," since from his experience, most Scandinavian dunked hard sugar lumps in their coffee and sipped on them.

In the olden days, women wore long-sleeved dresses with high collars. One spring there was an abundance of garter-snakes in the school yard, and of course, the boys enjoyed playing with them. One boy was showing others how to kill the snake by holding it by its tail and snapping it like a whip. Just as he was demonstrating this, the snake slipped from his hand and sailed away. At the same time, the teacher came around the corner of the school house, and the snake wrapped around her neck and slipped down the back of her dress.

Both the screaming and apologizing lasted a long time.

Another boy thought it would be fun to scare the teacher by making her think he'd hanged himself by tying the school bell rope around his neck. The box the boy used to stand on slipped. By the time the teacher got over her panic and managed to free the boy, it was almost too late. No one tried that sort of humor again.

Yet another boy came to school with an extremely black eye. When the teacher asked how he received his black eye, he answered, "I ran full fart into the door." (The Norwegian word "fart" means "force" in English.) The class erupted into uncontrolled laughter, and it took considerable effort for the teacher to gain control again.

A school picture was taken every year. Orval always made a funny face as the picture was taken (which reminds me of some other boys I know). Orval's mother was resigned to the fact she'd never see a normal-looking picture of her second son.

During lunch hour in the spring and fall, the boys liked to rush down to the river for a quick swim before having to get back to class. In the winter time, they'd slide down the river bank on the ice.

Wannaska School, June 1928
Back, third from right: Ray Mortensen;
second row, second from right: Orval Mortensen; right end: Leland Lee
Third row, forth from left: Ardythe Mortensen;
seventh from left: Lila Mortensen; eighth from left: Eddie Mortensen
Front row, third from right: Bennie Mortensen

࿐

The Mortensen farm was a mile south and east of Wannaska. When Ray was four years old, Andrew and Julia couldn't find him anywhere on the farm. Someone found him in town where he was peeking in the window of the schoolhouse. Andrew was angry and spanked Ray (the only time Ray remembered being spanked). Strangely, when parents are worried about their children and the fear is resolved, the parents are angry with the children). Ray never left home that way again.

Ray was a good student in most subjects. Learning was easy for him, especially spelling. So easy that sometimes he didn't study the assigned lesson. One time, a word on the test was "enough," and Ray spelled it "enuf." When the test was returned, the word was checked for further study. Ray remembered thinking, "If one 'F' isn't enough for her, I'll give her two." When his paper was returned the second time, a note told him to look in his book for the correct spelling. After that, he always spelled the word correctly.

Each day after lunch—if the class behaved—the teacher read a chapter from a book like *Tom Sawyer*. Ray always enjoyed this reading time.

When the children played softball at school, Ray had to bat left-handed (though he was right-handed), because he was larger than the other boys. He wasn't a good batter because of the way he had to bat, so he never really cared much for the game. A few boys learned to play well, but most of the boys were kept busy at home with farm chores and didn't have much free time to play at sports.

During Ray's school years, his best friend was a boy named Melford Olson, who lived a ways between the schoolhouse and Ray's farm. They played together at school and explored the nearby woods together. In early spring they'd test the puddles of melting snow by wading into them, hoping all the time the puddles were not too deep for their boots. Invariably, though, the puddles were deeper than they thought, and–oh, oh–they had wet feet. They never gave up testing, though.

Students were expected to attend school for eight grades, but during the seventh grade if a student thought he could pass the State Board examination, he could finish school then. Ray did this during the seventh grade and passed, so his formal education ended at that time. He did not plan to attend high school. He thought he was going to be a farmer like his father and grandfather. Even though he never went on to school, Ray continued to read and study on his own for the rest of his life.

Before WWII, not many students went on to attend high school in Roseau, for a couple of reasons. Most of the boys felt as Ray did–they were needed to work at home, and they were just going to be farmers and thought they didn't need any more schooling. And it was not economically possible to afford to go on to school. Some boys missed so much time from school because they were needed for work at home that they didn't even finish grade school.

Students who wanted to go to high school had to live in Roseau during the winter and work for room and board. The distance was too great to commute daily, transportation was not reliable, and the roads too muddy or snow too deep.[8]

After WWII ended, families could more easily afford high school, transportation began to be improved, and education was looked on as more important. Beginning at that time, more Roseau High School graduates began to attend colleges and universities.

---

[8] The Casperson School from Wannaska is now at the Roseau Pioneer Farm and Village. See details at http://roseaupioneerfarm.com/index.php?page=buildings

Riverside Lutheran Church at Wannaska

The congregation of Riverside Lutheran Church was established in Wannaska in 1901 as a member of the Norwegian Synod. As you know, the Mortensen family was the sole family of Danish origin in the vicinity of Wannaska. To the great merriment within the Mortensen family, when the Riverside congregation celebrated the fiftieth anniversary of its formation, the original minutes were read:

"This congregation consists of thirty-seven souls and seven Danes..."

Early pastors lived in Greenbush and served several congregations between Pelan and Skime. They traveled by horse and buggy over rough and muddy roads. One pastor traveled the circuit on skies during winter time.

The first pastor was Pastor P.C. Birkelo, and the second was Pastor N.J. Njus. For the first few years, services were held in the school house, but in 1910 work began on the present church building, which stands on an acre of land donated by Pete Larson.

Because of the distances that a pastor had to travel to reach his various congregations, services most often were held at times other than what we nowadays think of as "church time." The pastor held early morning service at one congregation, had lunch, then traveled on to the next one, and then on to the next after that.

Over the years, improvements were made to the church building. The men gathered to work together, and the women served the lunches. Around 1926 a steeple was built. In 1939 a basement was dug and made part of the building. In 1960 a parsonage was built, and in 1988 additional Sunday school rooms and a fellowship room were built. There have been more improvements. Riverside Church is a very attractive church, nestled amongst spruce trees.

In the early days a group gathered to work on the church. One of the volunteers had a very bad habit of constantly swearing, and the others in the party wondered how long it would take for the swearing to begin and how the pastor would handle the problem. Well, it didn't take long. Ole hit his thumb with the hammer and began to swear a blue streak. The pastor finally said, "Ole, do you have to take the Lord's name in vain like that?"

Ole replied rather sheepishly, "I know, Pastor. I'm sorry, but blankety blank blank, it hurts like blank."

ঌ

Another pastor was driving back to Wannaska from Roseau and caught up with Sam, who was again under the influence. Pastor stopped his car and let Sam get in. Pastor felt he had to talk to Sam about his drinking problem. Pastor asked him, "Sam, don't you know you're going straight on the road to hell?"

Sam switched his pipe to the other side of his mouth and replied, "Vell, I don't know, Pastor, you're doin' the driving. I'm yust ridin' along."

ঌ

One year a neighbor who lived close to the church thought the Sunday School class should learn to read Norwegian along with their Sunday School lessons. She began teaching the different sounds the letter "A" has. The children giggled at the strange sounds that letter has in the Norwegian language. The class didn't last long. Most families did not think it necessary for their children to learn to read Norwegian; they were Americans now, and English was what should be taught.

ঌ

Ray's parents were married in 1914 at the Mortensen farm home. Pastor S.L. Tallecson came to perform the ceremony. He was recently married himself, and brought his wife along to the wedding. They arrived quite a bit earlier than necessary, so they decided to go for a walk in the nearby woods. Their return was delayed—they *said* they got lost. Anyway, the wedding proceeded without further delay.

It's a small world: Around 1950 in Aurora, Oregon, Ray was telling our pastor, Harvin Christenson, about what happened at his parents' wedding and mentioned Pastor Tallecson. Pastor Christenson said that Tallecson had been his roommate when they were seminary students. He said Tallecson returned one evening from a date in town, threw himself onto his bed, began to kick his legs in the air, and kept saying, "I've done it, I've done it, I've done it." When asked just what he'd done, Tallecson replied, "I've found the girl I'm going to marry."

ঌ

For many years there was not an organized Sunday School in operation at Riverside, but when regular school was over for the summer, there'd be two weeks of Parochial School. Half-day classes were held in the school house for Bible lessons and Confirmation studies.

J. Earl Lee, a cousin of Ray's, was the Parochial School teacher one year, when he was a college student. Leland, Earl's younger brother, was disrupting the class. After several attempts to discipline his brother failed to achieve order, Earl finally lost patience and declared, "Leland, if you don't behave, I'm going to tell Mama." At that, Earl completely lost control of the class.

Earl Lee was six years older than Ray. When Earl was a young boy, he began taking piano lessons. Ray remembers the big box that the piano came in and how much Ray, Leland, and the other boys liked to play in the box. Ray wanted his parents to get a piano, not for the music, but for the box.

Earl became very proficient at the piano. When he came home from his university studies, he'd play a concert for his parents' friends and neighbors. Not many had any exposure to classical music, so they did not enjoy Earl's playing as they should have; but they were all proud of Earl and his accomplishments. He went on to become Professor of Music at Augustana Lutheran College at Sioux Falls, Iowa, and eventually Music Department chairman.

ꝏ

Confirmation in the Lutheran church was, and still is, an important time. The students studied hard for two years, memorizing the answers to the catechism questions so they could answer the pastor on their day of Confirmation. Mothers drilled the students at home, so each child was prepared to "read" for the pastor on lesson day. Most students became very attached to the pastor who confirmed them, because of this close time they spent together. When Orval was confirmed, one of his classmates was confirmed in the Norwegian language, because her father thought that was the proper language to use.

Ray always remembered his Confirmation Day with mixed emotions. He took his studies seriously and believed them, but on his special day, he was so nervous and afraid he'd make a mistake that it spoiled the real meaning of the day. What seemed to be the most important thing was not to make a mistake answering the pastor's questions.

Riverside Lutheran Church – 1959

In later years, as our children were confirmed, Ray was still a little nervous, remembering his own Confirmation. When customs concerning the examination of the confirmands changed, so that emphasis was placed more on re-affirming the student's baptismal vows than on how well the student could answer the pastor's questions, Ray felt much more at ease on Confirmation Day. He always trusted that the pastor knew whether the student was prepared for Confirmation.

For Confirmation, boys were finally allowed to wear long pants as a sort of rite of passage. Before this time, they wore knickers, which are pants that reach below the knee with elastic garters at the bottom edge to keep them from dropping below the knee. One time when Leland Lee was about five years old, he was outside playing with the cousins. He came into the house hurriedly for some reason or other, and when his mother noticed his pants leg dangling, she told him to fix it. Leland replied, "But Mama, my garter just won't gart."

ꝏ

Knudt and Annie Lee always sat in the front pew during church services. He'd often fall asleep and, much to his wife's chagrin, begin to snore quite loudly. Annie would jab him sharply in his ribs with her elbow. He'd be startled awake and exclaim, "Huh, what's the matter?" All the young boys, Ray included, found it very hard to keep from laughing out loud.

℘

One summer afternoon after a church picnic, the boys got into trouble with their mothers for laughing in church. The grass held an abundance of small garter snakes, and one boy put a snake in the back pocket of another young man, who was unaware of it. Later during the services, when everyone was standing (Lutherans stand a lot during services), the snake poked its head from out of the pocket and slowly looked all around and then slipped back down into the boy's pocket. The other boys, standing behind, couldn't keep from snickering.

Social Life in Wannaska

Fourth of July picnic, Otman's pasture in Pencer, circa 1925
Back, left to right: Ed Otman, Morten and Hilda Mortensen, Julia Mortensen, Mrs. Otman and baby, Andrew Mortensen, Ester Torfin, Grandpa Mortensen
Front: Orval, Ray, Elmer and Morriel Mortensen (in cap), Lila Mortensen, Bennie Mortensen, Bennie Torfin, Dorothy Torfin, Eddie Mortensen

Wannaska Party Line

In the early 1900s, telephones were installed in and around Wannaska. In those days, conversations were not as private as our phone conversations are now. Telephone customers were connected by a "party line," which is one line extended to all the customers. Each party heard everyone else's telephone ring. Each party had a special combination of long and short rings.

The equipment was enclosed in a wooden box that had a crank on one side of it. By turning this crank a certain number of times in long or short intervals, you'd reach the person you wanted to call. If more than the person called lifted their receiver when the phone rang, the sound of the caller's voice would be weaker, and those toward the end of the line had a difficult time hearing. This "listening in" was also called "rubbernecking" and was frowned upon. One central operator who was suspected of listening in always denied it; but one evening her husband came home late and found his wife asleep, sitting by the telephone with the receiver propped by her ear.

Church Suppers and Ice Cream Socials

In Roseau County, as in most small towns, church suppers were very popular. Social life centered around the church, and those suppers meant good food at a very reasonable price. The women of each church tried to outdo all the others. Over the years, attendance at the suppers at Riverside Church was always outstanding, because those ladies had the reputation of being among the best cooks in the county. People came from miles around to Wannaska for their suppers.

The Riverside ladies earned that reputation because of the thinness of their lefse, the consistency of their lutefisk, the tenderness of their pie crust, and lightness of their cakes; Riverside cooks excelled in every category. The ladies worked so hard preparing enough food for the large number of visitors to their suppers that some of the men thought the women worked too hard, and suggested they should just donate to the church the cost of the supper. Ray's father thought that way, but the ladies did not agree. I think they enjoyed their reputation as being good cooks, and I also think the men didn't understand the pleasure of the good attendance and the praises they received from the people they served. All might not have received the same appreciation at home.

At several suppers, one woman would bring a cake to the church, but she'd secretly hide it so it wouldn't be served. After the supper, as the kitchen was being cleaned up, all of the sudden she'd bring out her cake and say, "Oh, we forgot to serve my cake. I'll take it home for Ole." Well, after this happened a few times, someone decided to watch where the woman hid her cake, then took it out, cut it up and served it. When the woman went to get her hidden cake, lo and behold! It was gone! That ended the cake-hiding.

ꝏ

Potato Lefse

4 C cooked and riced russet potatoes
1/2 C half-&-half
1/2 cube butter
1 teaspoon salt
2 teaspoon sugar

Mix with electric mixer. The result is very dry. Refrigerate overnight.
Mix 2 C of potato mixture with 1 C flour.
Knead until well mixed and not sticky.
If not rolling right away, refrigerate again.

Roll 1/3 C of potato + flour mixture as thin as possible into a round pie-crust shape.
Use as little flour as possible to avoid sticking.
A lefse roller with ridges works best.

Bake on 450° griddle, moving it so it doesn't stick.
Flip when lightly brown.
Remove, fold, and cover with waxed paper.
Wrap in a dish towel to keep fresh.

ꝏ

Ice cream socials were always a big success in the summer time. Mothers would prepare a big picnic lunch. The day would usually be hot, and the kids could hardly wait for the ice cream to be ready.

The older boys took turns turning the big, ten-gallon barrel, which would be very hard to turn when the ice cream began to freeze. The boys took a lot of pride in showing off how strong they were, and the younger boys were anxious to be big enough so they could take their turns. Afterwards, there'd be games like baseball or horseshoe pitching or just good fellowship. These days made for lots of good memories.

ഗ

The Fourth of July was always eagerly anticipated. Early in the morning the boys started shooting firecrackers, so the Mortensens' dog Sport spent the rest of the day under the house. Later there'd be a picnic in town, with speeches, lots of good food, visiting among neighbors, and probably a baseball game.

If a man didn't take off his hat when the flag was carried by, he'd be told in plain talk that he'd better take it off. A constable was chosen for the day, usually Ole Larson, to keep the celebration from getting out of hand. All the young boys liked to watch Ole, because he usually was the one who had too much to drink before anyone else.

Baseball in Wannaska

In the days before radio, television, fast cars, and good roads, entertainment centered close to home. In the summer time, most towns had a baseball team that competed with each other enthusiastically.

One summer an umpire for the local team was cross-eyed, which led to more arguments than usual about whether a pitch was a strike or a ball, or if the runner was out or safe. At one confrontation, the batter angrily told the umpire he wasn't looking in the right direction. To which the umpire, also angry, and looking the batter in the eye, asked, "How do you know which direction I was looking?"

The Warroad baseball team, composed of Native American players, had two brothers, the Dumas boys. Their father was an excitable fan of the team, and would yell at his boys, "Come on, you smoked Swedes, play ball."

As a young man, Ray's cousin Lloyd Sorter played baseball for Wannaska. He took the game seriously and was a good player; he could tell after a couple of innings where in the field the batter would hit the ball. He'd shift his position in the field accordingly and be where the ball came, which was disconcerting to the opposing team.

Lloyd was annoyed with teammates who drank too much the night before a game or showed up for the game under the influence. Lloyd never drank liquor—he'd seen how it affected the family when his father had too much. The family was convinced that if Lloyd had lived in a larger city, he'd have been able to play league baseball.

Hockey in Wannaska

From freeze-up time in the fall until thaw time in the spring, ice hockey went on all the time. Boys—and sometimes girls, too—could skate almost as soon as they walked. The larger towns such as Roseau, Crookston, and Thief River Falls had hockey teams that exchanged games. A few close-by Canadian teams such as Fort St. Francis and International Falls also played Roseau County teams.

If you think baseball is an intense game, in northern Minnesota hockey was even more so. There'd be fights on and off the ice between players and spectators alike. Some people thought what made a great game was how many fights occurred.

In the mid-1930s Ray and several other young men constructed an ice-skating rink in Wannaska. They worked hard to make it nice for their friends and neighbors to have a place close to home to enjoy skating. They even built a warming shed, so skaters could warm up after being out on the rink.

Even though Prohibition was voted out in 1932, there were still moonshiners around the area, who made and sold whiskey without paying the required federal tax on it. To avoid detection, the illegal liquor was usually made at night, with the moon being the source of light, thus the name "moonshine."

One evening at the skating rink, a local moonshiner was there, too. The people who drank the illegal whiskey did not criticize the activity, but this certain person sold quite a bit of his whiskey to under-aged boys. That activity was not acceptable to other adults. Ray and his brother were so upset when this person was active around the rink that they got into a fight with him. Ray and Orval were still upset about this when they came home, their voices quite loud as they continued to discuss the matter. The noise upset Ray's mother and sisters, since they knew nothing at the time about what the problem was.

In later years, Ray's conscience bothered him about the incident at the hockey rink. On one of his last visits to Wannaska, he went to see the person with whom he had the trouble, to ask his forgiveness. The other fellow said he really didn't remember it. Ray felt better after talking to the man, anyway.

Dances, Fairs and More

At the turn of the twentieth century, after settlers came to Roseau County, the families gathered at each other's homes for entertainment. These house parties were popular and, as in Iowa where the Mortensen family served as popular hosts for these parties, so it was around Wannaska. Everyone liked to come to the Mortensen home. There'd be dancing, card playing, and good eating at these parties.

In later years, at one party in the summertime, friends gathered and food was being prepared; babies were sleeping upstairs. During summertime, heating stoves were removed from the house and a fancy plate placed over the pipe opening in the chimney to keep out soot and dirt. One young man thought it'd be fun to see what happened if he dropped a firecracker down the chimney. The commotion he caused was considerably more than he imagined: babies were screaming, with angry mothers trying to soothe them. The explosion pushed out the plate over the stove hole, covering Julia's clean house with soot.

Barn dances were popular throughout the countryside. Just about every community had a barn or hall for these dances. For years, the Berger family supplied some of the best music around. Violins, banjos, guitars, accordions, and some wind instruments had folks whirling around the floor. Later, Lois joined the Berger family when she married Emrance Berger.

Sometimes more liquor was consumed than should have been, leading to disputes between some dancers. One fellow, Ole Larson, thought he could beat up anyone in the place, when he had imbibed a bit. He wasn't a very big man, and some of those watching him thought he looked like a bandy rooster taking on the bigger roosters. He never really hurt anyone, just caused amusement at the dances. In those days, it was just the men drinking. Women did not drink in public.

Grandpa and Grandma Mortensen liked to attend the dances at Grefthen's hall up town. Grandpa liked polkas, schottisches, and other old country dances. Ray believed that Grandpa was an excellent dancer, the faster the better. Grandpa didn't care for modern ballroom dancing, because he thought that dancing close together was too suggestive.

ℰ𝒪

In the 1920s and 1930s, vaudeville shows came to town at times. Lots of people came to watch the show. One group that visited Wannaska was called Big Ole and delighted everyone with jokes about Scandinavians. The audience loved those jokes, in the same way Ray loved the little books with Ole and Lena jokes—even laughing in his last days, when his daughter Christine read aloud from an Ole and Lena book.

Before motion pictures began to be shown, and before electricity came to northern Roseau County, traveling lantern-shows visited the town. A light behind the film projected the image onto a screen. When moving pictures began to be shown, the reels had to be turned by hand.

ꙮ

Neighbors came to town when a traveling evangelist came to preach. A large tent was put up, filled for seating by using planks across nail keys. Most of these preachers were of the Pentecostal belief, and they always had an altar call after the sermon. Grandpa Mortensen liked to attend the services, but did not follow the ones who answered the altar call, because that was not the custom in the Lutheran Church. The preacher made a point of challenging Grandpa's Christianity because of his not coming to the altar, which upset Grandpa.

Occasionally those revival tent meetings got a bit out of hand emotionally. One fellow who was not very popular with the girls really enjoyed those services. When asked why, he said it was the only time he could hug a girl.

ꙮ

At County Fair time, lunch baskets were packed, everyone was loaded into the car and off they'd go to Roseau for the fair. The children were given about fifty cents to spend any way they wanted. In those days, fifty cents went much farther. Ray remembered the day at the fair as just the most wonderful day of the year.

One year as the family was on the way to the Roseau Fair, a wheel came off the car and continued rolling down the road. Quite a disastrous way to start the day. They eventually got the car fixed and went on to the fair. Years later, a group gathered, talking about different experiences, with Annie Erickson Sjoquist telling about the funniest thing she'd ever seen. Her family was on their way to the Roseau Fair when a car wheel rolled on past them. After the laughter died down, Orval quietly said, "That wheel was from my dad's car."

Ray thought the Roseau County fair[9] was much bigger and better than the Oregon State fair, showing more agricultural exhibits. The Oregon State fair was more urbanized by the time Ray attended.

The Roseau-Times Region

The Roseau County newspaper started in August 1982. The *Roseau-Times Region*, printed weekly, was always welcomed by its readers for its news of local happenings, farming information, weather, church and school events. Inside were reports from each of the many small towns.

Each town had a correspondent who reported the local happenings, such as church and school events, even who visited the previous week. A correspondent in Pencer wrote a very interesting column. After readers saw what was on the front page, they always looked to see what was in the Pencer news. Robert Wicklund had an intriguing, humorous way of writing about homey subjects, like his cat or the weather.

The newspaper stayed popular with Roseau County people who moved west. Those who subscribed passed it on to their family members or friends who didn't subscribe. They enjoyed keeping track of what was going on back at their former homes. We subscribed for many years, until there were so many new people in the news and so many old timers passed on, we didn't know the people mentioned.

In winter 1995, a headline said, "It's getting warmer." And alongside was a picture of a thermometer reading 30 degrees below zero. The week before, the temperature was more than 40 degrees below zero. Ray often said that after a very cold spell, when the temperature rose even a few degrees, it seemed warmer–still cold, but noticeably warmer.

The paper had a column noting events that happened Ten Years Ago, Twenty-five Years Ago, Fifty Years Ago, and so on. One week an item in the history column was about Ray's mother. It seemed Julius Westling had accidentally shot himself in the arm. While he was trying to get help, he met Julia Olson and Jeanette Thompson, who helped to get him to a neighbor's place. The family knew nothing of this event until reading about it in the paper–since Julia was a good Norwegian and never bragged. When the children asked their mother about it, Julia said only, "Yes, I helped him."

---

[9] See Roseau County Fair history details at http://www.roseaucountyfair.com/history/

ஐ

II: Mortensen Family and Farm Life

5: Life on the Mortensen Farm

The Mortensen farm house was large, with a kitchen, a living room, one bedroom downstairs, and two large bedrooms and one small bedroom upstairs. One of the large upstairs rooms became known as "the junk room" after it wasn't needed for a bedroom. It was used to store things not immediately needed, and also was used for cousins to play in during family dinners and parties. Our children played in the junk room with their cousins when we visited the farm.

The large upper bedroom's windows overlooked the driveway, the creek, and the field to the west. This room had a grate in the floor to let heat from up from the living room below to warm the bedroom. When Ray and his brothers lived at home, this was their room. The Mortensens had many visitors, who sat in the living room drinking coffee and telling stories–sometimes ghost stories. When it was the boys' bedtime, they hated to have to go to bed, so they'd listen beside the grate to the stories told below. Our children did the same when we visited.

In the downstairs bedroom closet, a floor board could be removed so a person could get into the cellar dug out of the dirt under the house. This was where Julia stored her canned fruit and vegetables, cabbages, potatoes, and other vegetables. Food did not freeze if stored there.

The house was formed like a "T" with an entryway into the kitchen from both the east and the west. These entryways served as a barrier from direct wind and snow. The one on the west was used to store boots and jackets, and the other one had shelves to store kitchen stuff and baked goods that needed to be saved for later use. The entry way on the west side was always used as the entry into house. Also on that side of the house between the downstairs windows was a hop plant that grew each year all the way up the side of the house.

In winter, the fire in the stove in the living room was banked high so the fire wouldn't go out completely before morning. The door between the living room and the kitchen was closed at night, and the fire in the kitchen stove died. The water in the bucket kept by the kitchen stove froze by morning, but soon warmed up after a fire was started. The wood box in the kitchen was always filled before going to bed, and there'd be enough kindling nearby to get a good fire started.

The front of the house faced the road. Grandpa Mortensen planted two rows of spruce trees, about six in each row, leading to the door at the front of the house. This door was rarely used, and no porch was built there, but the door was opened sometimes in the summer. These trees grew to be tall and impressive.

Farm Work through the Seasons

Andrew Mortensen with Lois
with Sport and the horses Dolly and Dandy

Spring on the Farm

The Mortensen farm consisted of about 200 acres; sometimes more acres were rented. Usually about 100 acres were planted in crops, the rest in hay. The farming practices followed a seasonal schedule.

The snow was usually gone by late April. The ground firmed up from the winter's moisture and field work could be started. Often rocks that kept coming to the surface had to be cleared before the ground could be plowed.

A good team of horses could plow about an acre a day, working from about six in the morning until noon. They were given an hour to rest, and then worked until about six in the evening. It was important that the horses be given enough rest. After the farm acquired a tractor in 1937, the work day was extended as long as daylight remained. The horses were still used a lot, even after a tractor came to the farm.

Sometimes the horses were spooked and ran away while working. This happened to Ray one time. The team finally ran into some brush that stopped them. After a lot of commotion, and some swearing, everything got under control again.

Crops were rotated on the Mortensen farm, in sets of about 20 acres at a time. They'd start with alfalfa, then the next year plant wheat (a main cash crop). In the following year they'd plant barley, and then oats, and then back to alfalfa. Flax was another good cash crop, planted for its oil. In the 1930s soy beans began to be planted for oil, replacing flax. Sweet clover was another good crop, with an odor that farmers like Ray enjoyed. Canadian thistle and sow thistle were the worst weeds that grew along with the seeded crops.

Each spring fish swam up the Roseau River to spawn. There was no limit on the sucker fish, and folks gathered large amounts to salt down for later use. These fish were bony but, when taken out of cold water, did not taste too bad. Wall-eyed pike and muskies came to spawn also, but only a limited number of these could be taken.

Summer on the Farm

When school was finished for the year, Ray and the boys got very short haircuts from their father and went barefoot for the entire summer.

Haying time was usually late in June. The grasses grown were alfalfa, timothy, and red clover. To feed all the stock through the winter, about two and a half tons needed to be stored for each head of cattle and three tons for each horse. The family milked about fifteen cows, plus calves and young stock, and kept from four to seven horses, so they had to harvest over fifty tons of hay each summer.

The barn was large and was filled first, and the rest of the hay was stored in large stacks in the fields where it had been cut. Sometimes fields near Wannaska were rented for hay. These stacks would be moved home in the winter.

During haying time, mid-morning and mid-afternoon lunches were brought out to the field. At other times, the men came in from the fields for those lunches and at noon time, also.

Haying time
Lloyd Sorter atop hay stack, Orval Mortensen below

ꟸ

Usually about twenty to twenty-five inches of rain fell each year. In dry years, sometimes the rain wouldn't be everywhere, just in strips. These light showers really helped improve the crops.

If the spring rains continued longer than usual, there'd be more mosquitoes, more bothersome than other years. There are several kinds, hatching at different times, so some mosquitoes might be bad early in the spring, and others might be present until late fall. Sometimes the animals were bothered by mosquitoes, which were out all day long, buzzing and biting, and annoying every living creature.

Two kinds of flies hatched in summer. Bull flies were a problem. They weren't around every year, but when they came, they lasted about six weeks. The other variety was black flies, and they were around almost every year. These flies bit people and animals. Sometimes they were so bothersome that horses couldn't be worked, because the flies caused the horses to be spooked and run away. These flies swarmed all over the buildings and were difficult to keep out of the house.

One year at harvest time, Ray was at a neighbor's home for dinner. Blueberry sauce was served in small dishes—and it was difficult to see the difference between the blueberries and the flies in the dish. A fellow worker told him later, "If it didn't move, I just ate." In those days, good manners meant you ate what was served, not to embarrass the cook.

ꟸ

Julia had extra work to do in the summer, besides her usual chores. She canned what fruit she could get. Places where wild strawberries, June berries, blueberries, and high-bush cranberries grew were scouted out over the spring and summer, and when each kind ripened, a visit was planned. Sometimes more than one family went on the picking party. All of these berries were small and a chore to pick, but the fellowship involved made for good times.

These berries were much smaller than the strawberries and blueberries we know. This small size made the flavor more intense. Ray often commented on how much better they tasted than the berries we have now. Perhaps they tasted so much better because of the short supply. Also, sometimes memory improves the taste.

One time Ida Aiken was out near the woods picking blueberries, which grow on short bushes in northern Minnesota. She was crawling on her hands and knees, picking away, when she heard a noise behind her and looked back to find a bear, also picking berries. Each was so startled, they went their different ways, getting away from each other.

After picking the berries, there was the work to preserve them for winter. Some were canned and served as "sauce," as it was called. Some cranberries were made into jelly.

Ray's mother had jelly to make and sauce to can, and also vegetables from the garden to can. Pickles had to be made—"slippery" pickles, pickles from watermelon rind, and of course, beet pickles. All this was done besides the regular chores.

One time during harvest at a neighbor's farm, Orval came in late for lunch. He thought the small dish of pickled beets near his plate was a dish of fruit sauce and proceeded to pour cream in the dish. The housewife and daughter noticed what happened and could hardly keep from laughing at Orval's mistake. He'd been taught to eat whatever was set in front of him, so he ate the pickles, cream and all.

Some vegetables, like carrots, were put down in bins of oats or sand. Because the oats or sand was dry, the vegetables would dry and keep for later use. Eggs were put down in bins of rock salt and preserved for baking later in winter, because the chickens did not lay eggs in winter.

ꝏ

Wood from poplar trees was used for the kitchen stove. This had to be cut in the summer to season, to be dry for winter's use. About fifteen cords were needed. This was stacked and, when it was seasoned enough, split to make a big pile out east of the house.

One year Julia had a new camera and took a few pictures of family members around the house. Once the film did not advance so a double exposure resulted, showing Ray chopping wood by a pile on top of the house. The family had a bit of fun over that picture.

The wood used in the living room stove was tamarack, which was cut during the winter as needed. This wood did not have to season, as it burned well soon after being cut and split.

When Ray was old enough, he took on the chore of chopping and stacking all the wood his grandparents needed.

Fall on the Farm

Harvest was usually started by late July, though each crop ripened at different times. The weather also had an influence on when certain crops ripened. The grain was cut by machine, and a binder gathered the stalks into bundles. These bundles were placed upright to cure, and the weeds and grass would wilt down and dry. If they didn't, the green growth clogged the threshing machine.

Threshing was an exciting time on the farm. Farmers expected a reward for all the hard work put in to raise the crops, colored by a concern for what the weather would be, and hopes that there wouldn't be any breakdown with the machines.

A crew was assembled. The steam-engine crew consisted of the engine man, a separator man, a water hauler, and a "straw monkey." This was the person—usually a boy too young to work at the other jobs—who'd drive a wagon filled with straw to be burnt in the engine to make the steam to run the separator machine. Orval said that was his first harvest job, and he felt proud to be working with the other men.

Whichever farm the steam-engine crew worked, they stayed at that farm until all the crop was harvested, boarding there for as long as it took. They'd be bedded down in the barn, or some in the house.

Sometimes the weather turned wet and delayed the threshing. If it rained too long, the grain started to sprout, which resulted in a bad harvest. Some years, the harvest was delayed until it snowed. When that happened, the snow was shaken off and the harvest would proceed.

The group that traded work with the Mortensens most years consisted of Lloyd Sorter and the Lees, Jensons, Williamsons, Bergstroms, and Emil Axelson and Adolph Dahlquist. This group usually did not board at each other's farm, except for the lunches and noon meals. Emil and Adolph always said the best place to thresh was at the Mortensens, because "Julia was the best cook in the country." This group exchanged work with each other at all their farms.

The day workers usually consisted of eight bundle haulers and two or three grain haulers. Each wagon had two men who filled the wagon with the bundles of grain. One man pitched a bundle onto the wagon, the other arranged the bundles to fill it evenly, and then they'd drive the filled wagon to the steam engine. Each would pitch the bundles straight, to not clog the machine. It was important to keep the machine running smoothly at all times.

When one wagon of bundles was emptied, another wagon was supposed to be there to be emptied. The men took pride in keeping their team working so as not to cause any slowdown for the crews.

Before WWII, a good yield for wheat was around thirty bushels per acre; now it is forty to fifty bushels per acre. A good yield for flax was ten bushels per acre; now it is fifteen to twenty.

ဢ

Young boys could hardly wait until they were old enough to be able to help in the fields with the men. When a young man was given a job with the threshing crew, it was a kind of rite of passage to manhood for him. Ray said he felt so grown up when he could keep up pitching bundles along with the other men. He was about fifteen years old when he could first work with grown men and not let the crew down.

One time Ray was working for a farmer who lived quite a ways from Wannaska. He was a German farmer and had different customs from the Scandinavians. When a Scandinavian is asked if he wishes to eat with you, he or she always says, "No, thank you." If the person doing the asking is also a Scandinavian, he or she will ask two more times. After the third invitation, it is then proper to say "yes" to the invitation. When the German farmer asked Ray if he'd like to eat dinner with the family, Ray politely replied, "No, thank you." The farmer said, "All right, then," and turned and went into his house for dinner, leaving Ray standing there hungry.

ꟿ

Mid-afternoon lunch at haying time, 1940s
Back, from left to right: Lester Olson, Orval Mortensen, Mildred Mortensen Simmons
Front: Grandpa Mortensen and Andrew Mortensen

While the men were busy in the fields, the farm wives were busy, too. After a big breakfast, a mid-morning lunch was prepared and taken out to the men. Then there'd be a big noon lunch, which really was as large a meal as the evening supper. A mid-afternoon lunch was taken out to the men, also.

Both noon and evening meals consisted of a couple of meat dishes, perhaps fried chicken and roasts of pork or beef, lots of potatoes and gravy, some vegetables, lots and lots of coffee, and then several kinds of pie. The mid-morning and mid-afternoon lunch was usually sandwiches, cookies, and jugs of coffee. A lot of bread would be available. All this meant the farm wife and older girls were busy baking the bread, cookies, pies, and cakes ahead of time.

Remember, all this cooking had to be done on a wood stove in warm weather. Also, the cleanup had to be done without running water, so the water had to be heated on the wood stove, too. Lois says it was exciting for the women. Everyone was in good spirits, lots of teasing and joking went along with the meals. The women felt good when the men expressed their appreciation for the good food served.

The family still remembers how embarrassed Julia was one time while feeding the threshing crew. A large bowl of gelatin topped with whipped cream was being passed around the table. One man's hands were very greasy, because he hadn't washed them before coming to the table. When he took the bowl, it slipped and turned over. He caught it with one hand under the whipped cream, turned it right side up, said, "Whoops," and passed it on to the next person, dirty cream and all. Julia didn't know what to do or say. She didn't want to embarrass the man, but she really wanted to take the bowl away.

℘

Julia Mortensen's Potato Salad for 100 People
20 pounds potatoes, cooked and sliced
1/2 C salt
3/4 tablespoon pepper
3/4 pint cooking oil
3/4 point vinegar
2 quarts diced celery
2 C diced onions
36 cooked eggs
1-1/2 quarts mayonnaise (Miracle Whip)
Sweet pickles and juice
Mustard and a little sugar may be used

℘

After combines came to be used, the grain was cut into swathes to cure. I first heard of this as "swatting" the grain. Not wanting to show my ignorance, I wondered what was meant by the phrase "swatting." Later I understood the diphthong "th" was not in Scandinavian languages, so the word wasn't "swatting"—it was "swathing." Quite a number of words with the "th" sound are pronounced with the "t" sound.

After the grain dried enough, the combine came and scooped up the grain, separated the grain from the stems, poured the grain into waiting wagons, and threw the straw to one side. Lois said it was disappointing for her when, after WWII, her cousin Leland Lee bought a combine that cut and separated the grain at the same operation. The combine driver was all the crew needed to harvest the grain, so there weren't a lot of other people around. It must have been a strange change of life for Julia, also.

ℰ

One summer a group of cowboys camped near the farm. They had a herd of wild, unbroken horses they wanted to sell. A lot of excited young boys in Wannaska thought they wanted to be cowboys when they grew up so they could sleep in tents, eat beans, and have a wonderful time with horses.

When Ray was small, he was fascinated with steam engines. He'd hurry home from school, change his clothes, and rush out to the fields to watch the machines and men work. His ambition in life was to be a steam-engine operator. Ray never realized his early ambition—by the time he was grown, steam engines were no longer in use.

Orval's ambition was to raise horses—and his dreams of horses came true when he raised his Belgians on his small farm near Canby, Oregon and showed them all over the Pacific Northwest.

Winter on the Farm

Mortensen farm in winter, 1940s

After the harvest, the house had to be readied for the cold winter that was coming. Storm windows were put in place. Tar paper was tacked on from the ground up to about three feet around the house. Bales of straw were stacked around the foundation, and horse manure was piled in between house and straw. Horse manure was used because it would heat and provide insulation from the cold. This didn't smell bad when the weather was cold.

The first snow arrived early in November. Sometimes the first snow melted before the real snow arrived. Sometimes the snow lasted until late April. Sometimes there'd be three feet of snow in the woods, but usually the wind blew the open fields free of most snow. I've seen pictures of the house and driveway showing at least three feet of snow.

In the winter, before roads were passable, the family went to church or to Roseau or to visit a neighbor in the sleigh pulled by horses. They'd bundle up in warm clothes, snuggle down under quilts and, with a large oven-heated rock at their feet, were quite cozy—if they hadn't far to go. When Ray and I were on furlough at Christmas time in 1943, we visited his parents. Ray hitched two horses to the sleigh, and we went out across the snow-covered fields to where Ray had built a shack on his small acreage. That was the only time I rode in a horse-drawn sleigh.

When real cold weather arrived, the family suffered fewer colds. Orval said that when he served in the Army in Greenland, everyone caught colds when the mail boat brought mail from home. When the children came down with a cold, Julia would rub their chests and backs with VapoRub, serve them a cup of hot lemonade, and then bundle them down under warm quilts. They'd sweat quite a bit, but would usually feel better in the morning.

Cold weather made special clothing necessary. The men wore long woolen underwear, woolen socks, and shirts. Wool was best for cold-weather clothing because wool sheds moisture without absorbing it. Orval said they wore three pairs of wool socks to school, because the floor of the schoolhouse was cold.

When the weather was really cold, the snow was dry and didn't melt. Then Ray wore felt moccasins that were very comfortable. He said it was almost like going barefoot. Of course, heavy boots were worn over them when going outdoors for long.

Woolen clothing was cheaper in Winnipeg, Canada, but a tax had to be paid when entering the U.S. Some of the old timers would go to Canada, buy several sets of underwear and shirts, put all of them on, and come back into the U.S. Obviously, this couldn't be done when the weather was warm.

Before it was customary for women to wear slacks, the women also wore long underwear and long cotton or wool stockings. But some young women for style sake wore silk stockings and short skirts when going on dates. One young woman had to wait outside by the roadway for her boyfriend to pick her up for their date. He was late, and by the time he arrived, the woman's feet and legs were frost-bitten. Quite a number of young girls learned not to be such a slave to fashion.

ꝏ

As winter progressed, care had to be taken that enough hay was readily available to feed the stock. When hay had to be hauled from stacks further from home, it was a difficult day's work when the snow was heavy. After the boys were more grown, Andrew had a much easier time hauling the hay.

The weather played a big element for when hay could be brought closer to home. On a good day, Ray and his father could haul three loads of hay from as far as Wannaska, but if the weather was too cold, the horses couldn't work that much. There was always the fear that there wouldn't be enough hay to last through big storms.

The meat to be used during the winter was butchered in the fall.

Lloyd Sorter and Orval Mortensen
Hunting, 1930s

February or early March was the other time for butchering for the coming summer's consumption. Orval said that was when the meat factory got busy. Pigs supplied the next year's hams, sausage, and bacon. The smoke house between the house and the barn was well used: beef was dried, smoked, and canned in the form of hamburgers, meat balls, and stew meat. There'd be plenty of meat during the summer, but when fresh meat was butchered in the fall, everyone was glad to eat something besides smoked and canned meat.

It took a lot of butchering to feed the Mortensen family. Andrew was not the typical butcher. He didn't like to saw down a hog's ribs for thin pork chops. He'd use a knife and a hatchet to cut between the ribs, which resulted in very thick pork chops. The family did not mind that when Julia served them so deliciously for dinner.

When Ray was still in the army and we lived in Battle Creek, his folks sent us a large dried and smoked roast of beef. It was welcome, because meat was rationed and scarce.

Winter Holidays

To get ready for Thanksgiving, Christmas and New Year's, Julia had lots of cooking and baking to do. There were the usual Scandinavian foods: fattigman (poor man's cake), krumkaka, rosettes, spritz cookies, and berlinkranser cookies, and of course, lots of lefse. I marveled how she could put these treats away and keep them until needed without two-legged varmints getting into them.

When I make some of these foods, I feel very close to Ray, because I recall how much he enjoyed them. I am so thankful he taught me how to make lefse and other treats.

Each of the holidays meant a big dinner to be served, with a turkey or a goose, plus all the trimmings. I was introduced to the treat of fattigman when we visited the farm while on furlough in 1943. The Christmas dinner was complete, as far as I thought, but after the pie was served, the dishes were cleared away, and more coffee poured, a huge platter heaped with what looked like pieces of pie dough was brought to the table. I was immediately captivated with this delicacy, and I am pleased to serve this for my family.

On Christmas Eve, the Scandinavian custom was for the family to be home together. Even the ones that might be inclined to drink too much and maybe neglect their families were all home on Christmas Eve. As another Scandinavian Christmas Eve custom, the cows and horses are given a little extra grain that evening. We kept that custom when we had stock or small animals.

Christmas Day began with church services, then a big family dinner. During the rest of the holidays, it was time to visit neighbors and be ready to entertain visitors. This kept on the whole twelve days of Christmas. The children liked the big dinners, mainly because of the custom of the adults eating first (different from the custom nowadays), then while the adults visited together in the other room, the kids got to eat—whatever they wanted, as much as they wanted, and no one said anything. Ray said one time he ate a whole pie, and no one told him "no."

Sears-Roebuck and Montgomery Ward mail-order catalogues were used by every family to receive items not usually found in Lee's Store or at stores in Roseau. The winter when Ray was eight years old, he became concerned because the family's order for Christmas presents had not arrived. The nearer the holiday came, the more he worried. When he asked his father about the order, Andrew passed the concern off, commenting about maybe the store being too busy to send the order on time. Ray stormed around, saying they should never buy anything from them again, and if he could, he'd do something really bad to them. Christmas Eve arrived, and there were presents for everyone. The order had arrived much earlier and been kept secret. Ray told the story often, laughing at his younger self.

ꕥ

The young people of Wannaska liked to have sleighing parties. One time Ray was driving the horses on such a party. He stopped the team to let off some of the riders. One of the persons getting off the sleigh was very pregnant. Just as she stepped down, one of the horses moved, which caused the woman to fall. She delivered the baby later that night. Everything went well, but Ray felt responsible for the early delivery.

During cold weather, the Northern Lights appeared, a phenomenon in the northern latitudes. They are bright colored lights that swish and swirl and swoop high in the sky at night, sometimes with sound. For centuries these lights could not be explained, with many associated legends. Scientists now explain them as electrically charged particles.

Ray's cousin Archie liked to tease his younger cousins, telling them they had to be careful, because the lights might swoop down and snatch up little kids. One time when he, Ray and Orval had to go out to the barn to feed the calves, the lights were flashing, and because of what Archie had told the boys, they kept close to him as they all hurried back to the house. Ray and Orval were really scared. Archie had not made up the story—it was a legend that also emigrated from Scandinavia.

In winter time coyotes hunted rabbits in the field to the west of the house. The window on the boys' room faced this field, and they could hear the coyotes yipping and yapping at night. Ray said, "When I was young, the sound of those coyotes made the hair stand up on my neck." He snuggled deeper under the quilts to keep from hearing the howls.

༄

In 1959 Ray wanted our family to see what Christmas was like in Minnesota. We took the train—because a few weeks before we were to travel, I saw a show on TV about the Donner Party getting stranded in the mountains on the way to California, so I was afraid to drive. The highway we'd have traveled was alongside the train tracks, and we saw that the road was perfectly dry all the way to Minnesota. I was reminded of this for a very long time.

Christmas at Mortensen House, 1954
Back, left to right: Mildred, Orval, Ardythe
Front: Julia and Andrew Mortensen

When we arrived at the farm, there was hardly any snow. It rained, filled up the ditches, and then froze, so our daughter could try ice-skating. Ray was quite disappointed that the family did not see a lot of snow, though we were chased by a big storm all the way home.

We did get to see the Scandinavian custom of Christmas Fooling that year. People came to the house one evening dressed in costumes to keep us from recognizing them. They teased everyone there, playing tricks, saying ridiculous things, and just plain being goofy. All the time, the family tried to guess who they were. Finally Julia set some refreshments out, which everyone enjoyed. Then before going home, the visitors revealed their identity (they were well-known to Andrew and Julia).

ꝏ

Fattigman – Poor Man Cookies
6 eggs
6 tablespoon sugar
6 tablespoon cream or half-&-half
dash of salt
1 teaspoon vanilla
3-to-4 C flour

Combine ingredients. Roll small portions at a time until very thin. Cut in diamond shapes. Slit center and pull end through. Deep fry in hot oil until golden. Drain on paper towels.

Andrew's Principles

Andrew, Ray's father, was a hard-working farmer. He learned good farming practices from his father, was kind to his animals, and was as good a horse-trader as his father had been.

Andrew was a good citizen. He participated in local affairs by serving on the township board for many years and also was treasurer for the church for several years. He was a very honest man.

On the farm, gasoline for farm use was kept in a separate tank and was not taxed. Although some families used the farm gas for personal car travel, Andrew never did. One time when Ray was going into town, he began to pump gas from the farm-use tank into the family car. Andrew came out to the car and said, "Ray, I know we're poor but we aren't so poor we have to steal gas." Ray felt really embarrassed, though he just didn't realize which gas he was pumping. Ray remembered this advice from his father, and for the rest of his life, he never knowingly broke the law.

In 1918 Andrew Mortensen bought a Ford Model T. While driving it home from Roseau, he slipped and turned over in a muddy ditch. Not a very good start with a brand new auto. After righting the new car, he continued home triumphantly. Later he tried to teach Julia to drive, but she didn't care to learn.

In 1938 Andrew purchased a Plymouth, and in 1947 a Dodge. When a tractor was brought home, everyone but Grandpa Mortensen was thrilled to have such a modern piece of machinery that would make their farm work easier. Grandpa never tried to operate the tractor, but continued using horses when he helped with farm work.

During WWII, gasoline and tires were rationed according to the amount of acreage or amount of production. Andrew received a notice that his ration of gas was being cut. When he inquired as to the reason, he was told his production was down. Andrew protested the decision, saying, "I don't think you are being fair. Yes, my production is down, but the reason for that is I have three boys in the Armed Forces." The ration board agreed and apologized. Lots of families had to rely on their girls to help with field work while their boys were gone.

Andrew had the notorious Scandinavian sense of humor. One rainy day he was in the house just after lunch when a peddler came to the door, offering to restore photographs that had yellowed from age. He spent quite some time going over different photos and making different offers. This went on for more than a couple of hours. Finally, when Andrew's and Julia's wedding pictures were being examined, with a straight face Andrew asked the man if he could do a special job on the wedding picture. He said, "Julia was so anxious to get married, she forgot to wash her neck that day. Maybe it could be repaired." The man knew he'd been had. He slammed his books together and stormed out of the house. Julia was shocked, of course, but Andrew thought he'd had a very good time.

Andrew was usually even-tempered, but one day he got into an argument with someone up town. He became quite agitated, and when he and Julia arrived home, Julia said, "Andrew, I'm ashamed with you losing your temper like you did." Andrew replied emphatically, still a bit agitated, "I did not lose my temper. I was using it all the time."

Mortensen Farm, 1940s

The Farm Animals

Andrew lost his temper another time, over a turkey gobbler. Julia raised turkeys for extra money, and a gobbler began to harass and frighten her. When she told Andrew, he came over to see, and the turkey began to attack him. Andrew grabbed the bird by the wattles and the two of them began to go around and around the farm yard, with the turkey trying to get away and Andrew swearing a blue streak. "You think you are tough, do you? You blankety blank blank."

After Andrew turned the turkey loose, it never bothered Andrew again—but it continued to bother Julia, so the turkey had to go. Ray said turkeys are about the dumbest of all animals. In order to keep the poults from starving, shiny marbles have to be put in the feed trough along with the mash. When the poults peck at the marbles, they pick up a bit of mash, thus getting nourishment.

ഇ

One year the family had a problem with a young bull that had become sort of tame and was used to being around people. But as the bull began to mature, it turned out he wasn't to be trusted. Julia was alone in the house, and the young bull was loose in the farmyard. He came up to the house, snorted and stamped around, and looked into the windows on each side of the kitchen, and bellowed and bawled. This frightened Julia, but she didn't dare go outside to get help. When someone finally was aware of what was happening, the bull was kept under control so that wouldn't happen again.

A few years later, another young bull became difficult to handle, so Andrew decided the bull's horns had to be removed. With Ray helping, the animal was snubbed closely so he could not move. Or so they thought. When Andrew began to saw on the first horn, the bull threw himself to the barn floor. Andrew twisted the animal's head so he could continue. When the job was finished, Andrew gave the bull a slight push with his foot and told him to get up. The bull did not move. Andrew pushed harder.

He said, more harshly, "Get up, you blankety blank."

"Dad, I think the bull is dead," Ray said.

Andrew stood there, looking perplexed, realizing he'd been working on a dead animal. Then he said, "I guess we'll have to butcher him."

When Ray told the story, he said, "I wanted to laugh because of the look on Dad's face when he realized the bull was dead. But I knew it was not the time."

The resulting beef was neither the best tasting nor most tender meat.

ꟾ

The farm always had cats, but they stayed in and around the barn. They knew where to be at milking time, so they could catch a stream of milk aimed their way. When Lois was young, she persuaded her mother to let her keep a kitten in the house. A litter box was set up behind the kitchen stove. One time visitors were sitting at the table having coffee with Julia and Andrew when the cat relieved itself, making noises and odors. Julia was incensed, and the cat had to go back to the barn.

ꟾ

Sport, the cattle dog, was the best dog that ever lived—or so Ray and Orval claimed. If Andrew said, "Go get the cows, Sport," the dog ran out to the pasture and barked and nipped at the cows' heels until they started to the barn to be milked. In winter, when Andrew took grain to Roseau, it took most of the day. By evening, Sport would be waiting by the road. When he heard the sleigh turn off the highway about a quarter of a mile away, Sport ran out to meet Andrew.

When Ray's folks visited us once, they had another dog named Sport. While they were away, Sport was left to stay with Lloyd Sorter, Ray's cousin, a short ways down from Andrew's farm. When the folks returned from Oregon, Sport came back home the next day on his own. Somehow, he knew they were home.

ꟿ

For several years when horses did most of the farm work, the favorites were Pete and Barney, and King and Dick. Sometimes two or three other horses worked the farm.

Barney, King, Dick and Pete

Working Days at the Farm

Both Andrew and Julia worked hard at their chores on the farm. They both were up early in the morning, and a fire would be started in the kitchen stove every day, summer and winter, spring and fall. In the winter time, water in the bucket had to be thawed. Andrew milked the cows, fed and watered the stock, and prepared to do whatever needed to be done that particular day. There was always more work than time in which to do it.

Julia assisted with the milking until the children were old enough to learn. Then the milk had to be separated and the utensils washed.

Breakfast was prepared, then the dishes washed and put away. At least once each week, bread was mixed and set for baking later. Butter had to be churned. Other chores were many: scrubbing the kitchen floor every morning (on hands and knees); dusting the floors in the bedrooms (beds were made as occupants arose); shaking out small rugs; and emptying, washing, and replacing chamber pots.

Before indoor plumbing, a large crockery pot with a cover was kept under every bed to be used if it became necessary during the night to empty one's bladder. A trip outside to the privy was very inconvenient and also very cold during winter. Young people don't know the embarrassment you feel when you replace the lid with a "clink" that you are sure can be heard all over the house.

After the morning chores, it was time for the ten o'clock lunch. During haying time, mid-morning lunch was taken to the field. Then it was time to prepare noon lunch (much more hearty than we think of as lunch), and more dishes to wash. On bread-baking day, this was the time to shape and bake the bread and rolls.

Evening supper was very hearty, and then more dishes to wash. After supper there may be a time to relax and visit with each other, and then there'd be a snack before bed time. Usually there were six meals a day to prepare and clean up after. That may seem a lot to non-farm folks, but these were very hard working people, and in the winter time, they needed more nourishment than we do.

Some days it seemed Julia never left the kitchen, what with cooking, baking, cleaning, and washing dishes. A lot of water had to be carried into the house and then tossed out the back door each day.

ꟃ

Monday was the day to wash clothes. That meant rising extra early—4:00 or 4:30 a.m.—carrying bucket after bucket of water to heat in a tub on the wood stove, boiling the clothes, and then scrubbing them on the wash board in big tubs. Next came rinsing and wringing out the clothes. The clothes were fed between two rollers by turning a handle to press out most of the water, and then hung out on the line.

In summer time, laundry was a hot job. Winter time made the last step interesting. The clothes would freeze before drying. This seemed to leave them a bit softer when they dried.

In later years, after Julia's brother Bennie died and his homestead shack was moved to the back yard, clothes were washed out there. The water was heated on his old stove. At least the work didn't take up all the room in the kitchen.

When the boys were eight or nine, Andrew got Julia a washing machine. A lever was moved to agitate the clothes, so they no longer had to be scrubbed on the washboard. The boys helped their mother by moving the lever. Ray liked to lie on the floor and move it back and forth with his foot. Boys like to try different things.

The first time she used the machine, Julia got up earlier than usual on wash day. She was done before breakfast time. When Andrew—who thought he was making her day easier—asked why she got up so much earlier, she replied, "I can wash the clothes, and it won't interfere with my other work."

The next day after washing day was ironing day. The iron was quite heavy. I have a child's iron that a young girl would use to learn how to iron. It weights three pounds, and an adult's iron probably weighed a pound more. Usually two irons were used, with one heating on the wood stove while the other was used on the clothes.

As the family grew, of course the amount of clothes increased. All of the washing and ironing of the clothes was worked in with the usual chores of milking, cooking, and dish washing.

ꙮ

Julia baked bread at least once a week and that took most of the day, but other days she baked rolls or cookies or pies. Julia was a very good cook, and something good was always cooking on the stove. When Ray and his brothers and sisters were young, they thought it a great treat to eat bakery bread as a change from their mother's bread. In his later years, Ray laughed at how silly that seemed.

Whenever our family visits to Wannaska ended, Julia packed so many good things for us that our children started eating not very far down the road. We finished the goodies before we arrived home.

In a small cupboard in the lower part of the dish cupboard (the one Grandpa and Grandma Mortensen received at the celebrated shivaree), Julia kept left-over cookies or other treats, so that anyone who wished could help themselves. One time Julia made some doughnuts that weren't quite up to her usual baking. Ray found them and began to eat some of them (no one else cared for them). He finally ate too many and lost his appetite for doughnuts for quite some time.

ꟸ

Many neighboring families felt they had to sell most of what their farm produced, and kept only marginal amounts for family use. For example, they'd sell all the cream and butter they produced, and then use lard for table spread; as a result, they'd have health problems and dental problems.

Andrew and Julia felt their family's welfare came first, so they used all the milk, cream, butter, eggs, chickens, beef, and pork they wanted, and then sold the rest. They also tended a large garden—many neighbors didn't have gardens. Julia served lots of vegetables for meals, and canned or preserved for use in the winter. As a result, their family was healthier than some of their neighbors. During the Depression, in the large cities food was a problem for many families, but on most farms, food was not the biggest problem.

ꟸ

As the children grew out of their clothes, Julia made them over for the younger ones. She also made quilts with the left-over material, saving small scraps until she had enough to take to a woman who made rugs with them—and who always had dandelion wine to serve visitors.

Once, when Lois was three, Julia brought her along to visit the rug-making neighbor. Julia did not care to drink wine, but didn't want to hurt her neighbor's feelings, so she just set the glass aside. Lois drank it, unbeknownst to her mother, and probably sipped glasses of other visitors. After a while she started acting quite strangely, so Julia took her home. When Julia told Andrew about Lois, he watched her for a while, and then burst out laughing. "She's drunk," he said. Julia saw to it that this never happened again.

Julia oversaw the children in doing their homework, and also went over their Confirmation studies to be sure they knew their lessons well. Studying was done by the light of kerosene or gas lamps.

ꟸ

When Julia began spring cleaning each year, she was not a bit sentimental about anything. If she hadn't used anything for some time, out it went. Rugs were taken out, hung on the clothes line, and beaten hard. Closets and cupboards cleaned thoroughly. Every room was scrubbed clean, and then the painting and paper hanging began.

Ray said the only times he remembered his parents being short tempered with each other was during the annual house-cleaning jobs. Andrew helped with the painting and hanging wallpaper. He was very good at the job, but it took several people to help and they weren't always as good as he was, so he became a bit impatient with them.

A year after Andrew retired, he and Julia planned to hang wallpaper. Julia brought out the equipment for the job, cooked the paste, and was ready to go to work when a neighbor came by and took Andrew fishing. Orval said his mother was quite upset, having to put all the stuff away again.

Where we lived in Oregon, a friend of ours collected watches and old clocks. Ray mentioned that his folks had a couple of old clocks, so when Ray and his Uncle Jens planned a trip back to Minnesota, our friend Walt asked to go along, since he hoped to buy old clocks for his collection. When Walt asked Julia about her clocks, she said, "Oh, when we got electricity, I threw those old things in the trash." Walt was sick at the loss, but that was Julia—if she didn't need it, out it went.

Ray was extremely proud of his mother. He felt it was a miracle that she became the person she was, considering her girlhood experiences and the way she was raised; she had no mother to teach her the way other girls are taught, although her sister Minnie did what she could. Julia grew to be a good wife and helpmate, a wonderful mother, a great friend to others.

Hard Times in the 1930s

For several years, until the beginning of WWII, farm prices stayed low, and most farmers worried about meeting mortgage payments.

One summer day in 1937, a hailstorm came through the area. Within half an hour, an anticipated prosperous harvest was destroyed. Unless one has experienced a similar happening, it is difficult to understand the emotions of Julia and Andrew. Here, in the middle of the Depression, mortgage payments to make, a good harvest expected, and then to suffer this loss.

An hour later, Andrew was lying on the floor (his usual place to relax), reading a Zane Grey novel. Julia said, "Andrew, how can you be so uncaring?"

He said, "It wouldn't change anything to be excited."

Most people think the Depression started with the stock market crash in 1929, but for several years before then, prices for farm products had become low; as a result, money became scarce, mortgage payments could not be met, and banks began to foreclose on farms. Besides that, there was a severe drought for several years in the Central Plains, North and South Dakota, Nebraska, Iowa, Arkansas, Missouri, and so on. The wind blew top soil away, crops withered, and farmers were left without enough seed to plant the next year.

A lot of farmers in those states had to leave or starve. Those who stayed on their farms tried to find other jobs to earn money, but money-paying jobs were difficult to find. When a farmer needed help, he couldn't pay cash for help, but would trade work with another farmer. Those few who could wait out the drought were finally able to make a living again.

In addition to the drought, there were not enough trees to break the effects of the strong winds and erosion of the soil by over-plowing. The farms became more productive when some of these practices were corrected by planting trees, strip plowing, and rotating crops, along with more reliable amounts of rain.

Northern Minnesota did not suffer from drought as much as those areas further west or south. There was enough rain for crops to grow and there were still enough trees to keep the wind down, so the main way they suffered was from the shortage of cash. One winter Andrew had the contract from the Creamery to haul away the excess buttermilk every day, which was used with other feed for the hogs. When the hogs were large enough to be butchered, the carcasses were sold to the logging camps for three cents a pound. That was not very much money for a winter's work.

Many farmers from the Dakotas and Iowa moved into Roseau County, possibly because of family members living there, or because of mutual Scandinavian ancestry. Some started over and made a fair living, but some were so beaten by their experiences, they never could get going again. They just barely existed at jobs other than farming.

The Depression of the 1930s made a lasting impression on Ray. He was about fifteen years old when the Depression started and was aware of his parents' concern about not having money to make the mortgage payment, or having enough money for other things the family needed. When we moved to our farm in Hubbard in 1948, we had a short-term loan from a neighboring farmer. Ray worried until the loan was paid off, remembering when his parents faced the same problem. For the rest of his life, Ray paid cash for everything or he didn't buy, because he feared not being able to pay the debt.

When Ray finished grade school, he worked with his father and brothers on the farm doing the daily chores and working the fields. He was fully grown by his fifteenth birthday and strong enough to do a grown man's work. He was ambitious and wanted to learn about machinery, so in winter 1936 he attended automotive school in Fargo, North Dakota.

After school in North Dakota, Ray returned home and built a machine shop between the house and the barn, where he did repairs and a little blacksmithing. He also did woodworking, building his mother her first kitchen cupboard, which she used for as long as she lived in that home.

In the late 1930s, there was still a desperate need to earn cash. In 1937 Ray worked on a road crew that upgraded the highway from Roseau to the southern part of the county. He also worked for the local veterinarian, going with him from farm to farm to test the local cattle herds for brucellosis and tuberculosis, two serious diseases. Any animals discovered with these diseases had to be disposed of. Some farmers objected to allowing the vet to test their cattle, but the law was strictly enforced. Ray said some farmers didn't clean their barns very often. He and the vet had to duck their heads when they entered the barns. This made Ray shudder at the thought of such unsanitary conditions, as he was used to the clean barns his family kept.

In 1939 Ray bought 20 acres of land from Martin Aiken and built a tar-papered shack just large enough for a stove, a table and chair, and a bed. He spent the summer there, getting the fields ready for crops. He and a neighbor, Emil Axelson, had lots of rocks to clear away. In later years, Emil lived with his family in Salem, where he worked for a large bakery. Emil joined our church and often supplied much-appreciated cinnamon rolls. He often spoke about picking rocks with Ray.

Ray thought he'd live on this farm for the rest of his life, adding acreage to build up a large farm, but he needed money to buy machinery and other equipment. At this time, jobs were to be had on the West Coast. War had started in Europe; Germany had invaded Poland, France, Holland, and Belgium and was threatening to invade England.

Our government decided that England needed our help with heavy equipment, armaments, trucks and ships, and so on, so manufacturing plants expanded. Portland, Oregon was well situated for such industry, being on a large river near the ocean.

So Ray, his cousin Lloyd, and their friend Art Johnson left Wannaska in Lloyd's pickup. They traveled west, sight-seeing, camping out where possible. They came through Seattle, but didn't stay there because the city had too many hills, so they came on to Portland.

Upon arrival in Portland, the three found rooms in the New York Apartments on S.E. Seventh and Belmont Street. A large market was a block away and a movie theater was just a couple of blocks away, so everything needed was close by. Ray got a job in a foundry four blocks away. It was wonderful to finally be making money. The work at the foundry was very tiring at first, the heat hard to get used to, but Ray enjoyed the job and was promoted to more difficult duties such as pouring stainless steel, an intricate process. The foundry had contracts to make stainless steel port holes for the U.S. Navy.

The three men ate their evening meals at a nearby restaurant and on payday would leave the waitress a good-sized tip. They left a tip only on payday, but they received extra special treatment from her each night they ate there.

Ray and the others occasionally visited the nearby theater, The Oriental. When I visited my aunt and cousin on Sundays in that neighborhood, we'd go to a movie at the same theater and walk past the apartment house where Ray lived. We never met then, and probably wouldn't have paid attention to each other if we'd stood next to each other in line at the theater. It was not the time for us to meet.

Several men who worked with Ray at the foundry came from the Midwest. The boss there said he liked to hire farm boys, because they knew how to work.

Lloyd did not stay in Portland long, but returned to Wannaska. Art and Ray continued to room together until Ray received an order from the Roseau County Draft Board to report for duty in the Army. Instead of going back to Minnesota to report for duty, he reported to the Portland office.

When Ray told his boss he'd been drafted and would be leaving, his boss said that Ray should have told him sooner. Because Ray was working at a Defense job, he could have been deferred, but it was too late to change anything. Ray felt it was his duty to serve as he was called to do. Art continued to stay in the apartment. He worked in Portland for several years after the war, and visited us in Hubbard occasionally.

Grandpa Mortensen Moves Back to the Farm

In the fall of 1929, Andrew, Julia, Morten, and Hilda became aware of something being planned in the family, but didn't know what or who was involved. The men thought their older sister Annie was behind it and was not telling them. The four were put out about not knowing what was going on, and even discussed it amongst themselves, and said, indignantly, "Well, if that's the way Annie is going to be, she can go ahead, and we just don't care" (or words to that effect).

They were all embarrassed when the rest of the family put on a surprise celebration for their wedding anniversaries along with Grandma and Grandpa Mortensen's sixtieth anniversary. All the family came home to celebrate that anniversary, except Andrew's brother Jens, who couldn't raise the fare to travel from Oregon.

Jens and Ellen Mortensen, 60th Anniversary
Front: Jens and Ellen Mortensen
Back, left to right: Hannah Hardland, Christine Johnson, Morten Mortensen, Marie Hunking, Andrew Mortensen, Annie Lee, Martha Davis

After Grandma Mortensen passed away in 1941, Grandpa made plans to move back to the farm. While Ray was helping him to pack his things, Grandpa gathered up all his immigration and naturalization papers, opened the door of the stove, and threw all of them into the fire, saying, "Well, we won't need these anymore."

Ray was just sick whenever he remembered this, at the thought of the loss to the family of those papers.

When Grandpa moved back to the farm, he was still able to help a bit around the farm. He was easy to care for and kept himself clean. One time the radio was playing quite lively music in the living room, where Grandpa usually sat warming himself by the stove. Ray's mother came to the door and beckoned Ray to come to her. She said, "Didn't I tell you boys not to play music like that because Grandpa might not like the noise?"

Ray said, "But Mom, Grandpa is playing the radio." And Grandpa's foot was keeping good time to the music.

One day, Andrew told Orval and Ray to pump water to fill the stock tank. Being boys, and each not wanting to do more than the other, they didn't respond very rapidly. They argued with each other about who was doing the most, and the tank was not being filled. Grandpa Mortensen was nearby, helping for the day. Usually he did not interfere with any discipline matters, but he finally heard enough and said to the boys, "Your father said to pump!" Well, the boys really pumped water after that. They had so much respect for their grandfather, they wouldn't dream of displeasing him.

The creek that divided the farm was the cause of a worry after Grandpa Mortensen came back to live with Ray's parents. One spring day, no one could find him. Eventually he was found taking a bath out behind the barn in the creek. It was quite cold, but Grandpa didn't suffer any bad effects.

Grandpa died in October 1944. Ray, who called Grandpa the most important person in his life, described walking down to that creek, thinking about Grandpa and feeling it to be the most peaceful day of his life.

Grandpa Jens Mortensen, 1940s

&

6: Mortensen and Sorter-Olson Families

The Mortensen Children, 1928
Ray, Mildred, Orval, Ardythe, Bennie

Stories of the Andrew and Julia Mortensen Family

After Andrew and Julia were married, Grandpa Mortensen's daughters Hannah and Marie and his younger son Jens were still living at the family home. The Mortensen family was well known then (and still to this day) for their teasing of each other. Grandpa was quite strict about no one becoming angry if teased. But here we have a young bride, a very sensitive person who had never been around this sort of relationship before, who was reduced to tears in private quite a bit of the time. Some people might harbor resentment towards the ones who hurt her feelings, but being the very loving person Julia was, she never showed any bitterness. She had only love for this family for all of her days.

Andrew rented the farm until 1923 when he took out a mortgage to buy the farm. From then on, each year was a constant struggle to make the mortgage payments. Some years were quite successful while others were not. Three things had the most influence for favorable harvests: weather, yield per acre, and price per bushel, and all these items hardly ever happened at the same time. But that's farming.

Six children blessed the family of Andrew and Julia Mortensen: Ray in 1915, Orval in 1918, Ardythe in 1920, Bennie in 1922, Mildred in 1927, and Lois in 1936. English was spoken in the home because of the language difference between Andrew and Julia, and therefore none of the children learned to speak either Danish or Norwegian.

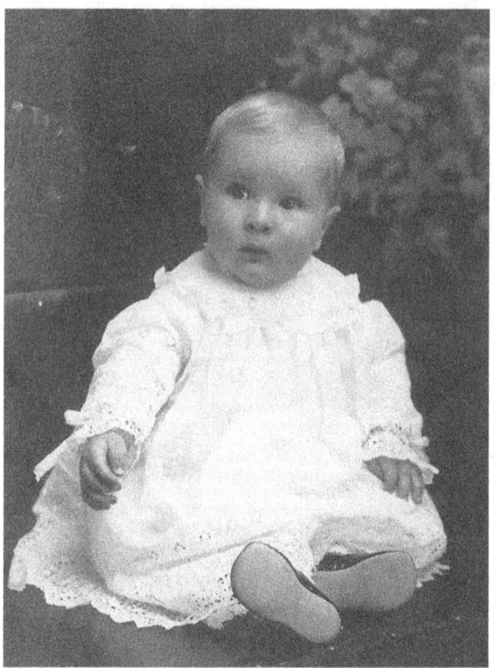

Ray Mortensen, 1916

Andrew was a very good father. He expected the children to mind their mother and not to talk back to her. If there was something Julia couldn't handle, Andrew would. His voice could sound stern enough, the children obeyed quite readily. Ray remembered only one spanking (when he went to the school without anyone knowing it), so discipline was just the children knowing what was expected of them, and they did it. When I visited, Julia told Lois and Mildred to bring the butter and cream from the well cooler. They began to argue which one of them was supposed to do that. Andrew finally said, "You heard your mother," and they immediately did as they had been told.

Andrew and Julia taught their children to be honest. Ray and his brothers and sisters taught their respective families the same lessons. Andrew was well respected by everyone who knew him. In those days, handshakes sealed decisions, and a man's word was his bond. Andrew thought when a person had been instructed for Confirmation, he knew right from wrong and was responsible for his actions after that.

ꟸ

From early in the morning until dark, there was always more work to do on the farm. They had no electricity; they used kerosene lamps and later white gas lamps. They had good water, but it had to be pumped from the well in the barn yard and carried into the house in buckets. The water well in the kitchen stove had to be kept full to heat. The bathroom was a privy at the end of a short path outside the house. Julia kept this as clean as possible, scrubbing it almost every day, and Andrew kept it white-washed each spring.

Ray was glad to be able to assist his parents in installing a bathroom inside their house during our visit in 1954. Two factors delayed installation before that time: one, the cost, and the other, the ability to prevent pipes freezing in winter. The indoor bathroom had other advantages besides convenience. In our exchange of letters several times a year, it was noted that the family suffered attacks of enteritis, but installation of bathroom and water facilities resulted in a dramatic decrease in the number of times this occurred. Using hotter water for washing and rinsing the dishes, changing the water more often, and removing the privy had positive effects on this problem. Julia kept a very clean house and used good hygiene practices, but the house needed indoor plumbing to stop the spreading of disease.

In 1918, when Ray and Orval were small, an influenza epidemic swept through the area. A lot of families were affected. Andrew and Julia were ill, and a neighbor, Ole Hall, came over to help with meals. He meant well and did the best he could, but the kitchen and the boys were not kept as clean as Julia kept them. Julia cried when she saw Orval's rompers and face dripping with prune sauce, though Orval didn't care. Later Aunt Annie came and took the boys home with her and cared for them until the family was well again. Neighbors were very helpful when a family had illness. The chores got done, with neighbors going from farm to farm, feeding stop and bringing necessities to the families that were ill.

Although there was always work to be done on the farm by everyone, Ray and his brothers and sisters had time to be young and enjoy themselves.

Ray Mortensen – Family Stories

Ray, 1918 – Caught with Grandpa's pipe

When Ray was old enough for a gun, Andrew carefully taught him how to handle it safely. Ray was warned that if the gun was left loaded, he'd lose the privilege to have it. Only one time did Ray forget to unload the gun when he left it in the entry way. When he regained the use of the gun, he was extra careful how he used it.

Minnesota had an over-abundance of gophers, so a bounty was offered for their demise. A County official paid money for gopher tails.

Ray was a good marksman, and the bounty money he earned paid for the ammunition he shot.

Some years, a large numbers of rabbits appeared in the fields and woods. Then, after a few years of over-supply, their numbers suddenly decreased because of disease; then in a couple of years, there'd be lots of rabbits again.

Ray spent lots of time in the fields, lying in wait for gophers to pop out of their mounds. He also liked to watch the mating dances of prairie chickens and the thumping of the grouse in the spring. On lazy summer days, he watched cloud formations in the sky and let his imagination run wild.

A creek divided the farm. In the early summer small fish were abundant enough to tempt Ray to try to catch them. He had just a pole and a string with a bent pin for a hook, but he'd patiently tease the fish to his bait. When he'd finally catch a few of them, his mother cleaned and cooked them for Ray to eat. To him, that was a pure Epicurean delight.

ꕤ

No big celebrations were held for the children's birthdays, but on their own day, each child did not have to do chores. Ray liked to celebrate his day by fishing. Fine, but one year he coaxed Orval to do the same on his birthday, so Ray could fish, too. That would have been fine, except Orval didn't care a bit about fishing; however, to please his brother, he went along with Ray's wishes.

When Ray was five or six, his cousin Archie made him a model steam engine with straps and turning rods, very realistic in detail. Ray was thrilled, and played and played with it all evening. He was entranced with it, and didn't realize how badly he needed to go outside to the privy. When he finally started to go out, he got as far as the back door, clutched the back of his pants and began to cry. Too late!

When Ray was about seven, he received a pocket knife for his birthday. He went to visit his cousins Archie and Lloyd, to show it to them. The time passed quickly and it began to get dark. Ray remembered that he straightened out his knife, held it out in front of himself and ran all the way home—about a mile away, with no neighbors between the farms. When he told this story, Ray said, "The knife was so dull it probably wouldn't cut butter, but I felt ready for whatever was out there."

One year Ray had some duck eggs he wanted to hatch, but no duck would take them, so he put them into a hen's nest. They hatched, and when the ducklings went swimming in the creek, the hen ran frantically back and forth, not understanding why her babies were in the water. One duck didn't go into the water soon enough and never learned to swim. Ray said it was so funny to see it turn upside down when it was placed in the creek. The duck had to be rescued before drowning.

Ray Leonard and Marjorie Louise Wright Mortensen

Orval Mortensen – Family Stories

Orval's favorite past time as a child was pretending to harness up and drive horses. He could spend lots of time going through the specific things necessary to properly hook up a horse to a wagon. He learned the process thoroughly: in his later years, Orval raised and showed Belgians in plowing and pulling contests in Oregon.

When Orval was about eighteen months old, he tumbled down the stairs. His father rushed to pick him up. When his mother asked if Orval was hurt, Andrew said, "No, he just bumped his head."

As a little boy, Orval was an early riser. He played hard all day and was ready for bed after supper. A lot of the time he'd finish his supper and fall asleep at the table with his face in this plate. He'd be put to bed, sleep all night, and then be up early, ready for another busy day.

Orval was older than most babies before he could walk–almost three years old. His father used to laugh and say, "Orval didn't see the need to walk until he wanted to chase girls."

After eating at a big family gathering, all the cousins chases each other around the big table, laughing and yelling and having a big time. One time while running, Orval fell, and his mouth came down on a leg of the oak table, loosening his front teeth. They eventually tightened up, but the marks stayed on that table leg for the life of the table.

Ina Erickson Wierschke and Orval Harold Mortensen

Ardythe Mortensen Fredrickson – Family Stories

As a young girl, Ardythe liked to play with her mother's kettle covers, measuring cups and spoons, like most little girls do. One Christmas she received a nice set of miniature dishes and kettles. She seemed to like them a lot, but a bit later her mother noticed the gift was neatly stacked and placed to one side, and Ardy was busy playing with the old kettle covers and cups again.

Mildred, Ardythe, and Lois Mortensen, circa 1939

Ardy had serious ear infections as a young child. They were very painful and, because antibiotic medications had not been discovered, recovery was slow. She'd have to stay in bed for long periods of time, and her mother tried many things to keep Ardy comforted. The favorite pastime was for her mother to read to her. She didn't have many books, so it became easy for Ardy to memorize them. If her mother missed reading any little word, Ardy corrected her. It had to be exact every time.

When Ardy was older, she became proficient at baking pies, but when told to bake pies for supper and she wasn't in the mood, she'd bang the pots and splash flour around, but the pies were always good.

When we were married, Ray told me that no matter how good my pies might be, they'd never be as good as his sister's. I don't think he meant that the way it sounded, because he never refused to eat my pies.

Ardythe Ellen Mortensen and Clifford Fredrickson

Bennie Mortensen – Family Stories

Ray's brother Bennie had pneumonia when he was a small baby. He was so sick and his breathing so weak, his parents placed a small mirror to his nose to determine if he was still breathing. It was a stressful time for the family before he fully recovered. Again, the lack of antibiotics caused this illness to be so very serious. There are so many illnesses that are not so serious nowadays because we have antibiotic medicines.

Bennie and Mildred Mortensen

As a boy, Bennie was involved with 4-H projects. He raised a pig that became quite tame because of all the attention Bennie gave it. When the pig saw Bennie across the farmyard, it would squeal and squeal until Bennie came and petted him or scratched his back. One day Bennie couldn't be found. Everyone looked all over, until he was found sound asleep on a pile of hay with his arm around the pig, and the pig sound asleep, too.

Naomi Adeline Rappé and Bennie Leo Mortensen

Mildred Mortensen Simmons – Family Stories

The night before Mildred was born, her mother had been bedding down all the threshers staying at the farm. When the men became aware of the imminent birth, Olaf Abrahamson, one of the threshers, said, "Guess there will be another place to set at the table for breakfast."

In later years Mildred and her husband operated a grocery store in Wannaska. Every time Olaf stopped at the store, he'd tell her, "I was at your folks' home the night you were born."

Mildred Mortensen Simmons

When Mildred, or Millie as she was called during her childhood, was about three or four years old, she came into the kitchen from the barnyard and told her mother, "Orval says we have a hell of a barn." Julia had a few words with the boys about being careful with their language around their sister.

Mildred was older when she had scarlet fever. Ray remembered how red her lips were while she was ill. The family was quarantined until she was no longer contagious. Before modern medicine, families were quarantined to prevent the spread of some illnesses. Being quarantined meant no one could leave the farm and no one could come into the house except family members who lived there. When supplies were needed, neighbors left them by the door.

Mildred Mary Mortensen and Russell Elmor Simmons

Lois Mortensen Berger – Family Stories

Ray, Orval and Ardythe were grown and not at home much anymore when Lois was small. She says she felt quite alone at times. When WWII came along, the family happenings and gatherings were different than when Ray was growing up.

When Ray was in the army, Lois wrote him letters. He was so glad to get them, he'd show them to his friends, and when we were talking about home and things like that, he'd read me the latest letters received from his little sister, so pleased that she'd written to him.

Emrance Lavern Berger and Lois Carroll Mortensen

Stories of the Sorter-Olson Family

The Sorter family—Julia's older sister Minnie, with her husband and sons—lived about a mile east of the Mortensen farm home. Uncle Abe was a jack-of-all-trades who did a number of jobs: a blacksmith, a carpenter, and a steam sawmill operator. Although Abe had a drinking problem, kids liked him. Ray said Uncle Abe was fun to be around.

Abe Sorter and Minnie Olson Sorter

Uncle Abe and Aunt Minnie had two sons, Archie and Lloyd. The boys were very close to Ray and his brother Orval. The boys liked to tinker and make things. One year Ray received a set of dominoes for Christmas that Archie and Lloyd had made. The pieces were about two inches by one inch by one-half inch, and the dots were burned into the pieces. Archie was among the first to build a radio, a single tube radio with head phones. Archie and Lloyd built a tractor with a two-horse-power hit-and-miss steam engine. It couldn't do much, but it was a lot of fun for neighbors to watch.

One time in the early days there was quite a bit of excitement when a young moose fell into Uncle Abe's well. Eventually Carl and Alfred Nelson, Uncle Bennie Olson, and Uncle Abe were able to raise the animal out of the well.

Abe Sorter family
Abraham, Archie, Lloyd and Minnie Olson Sorter

ꕤ

In 1928, a severe influenza epidemic hit the area, as well as the rest of the country. Practically every family was affected by it. Ray, who was fourteen, and other well persons went to the farms of sick folks and did their chores for them. Orval said there were some people who really didn't do much good for themselves in several ways, but when others were in need—a new baby or illness—then they'd be amongst the first to come to the aid to those in need.

Among the many deaths were Uncle Abe and Archie. Aunt Minnie was so ill that she wasn't told of their passing for several days. Andrew and Julia were ill also, as was Mildred. Julia insisted that she had to go to the funeral, but Aunt Annie spoke sharply to her, saying, "All we need in this family is another death. You stay right in bed."

The epidemic was so bad that gatherings inside of churches or other such buildings were prohibited. There were so many funerals in the very cold weather that not many people attended the outdoor services. Ray, Orval, and Grandpa Olson were the only family members able to attend the funeral for Uncle Abe and Archie. Both Ray and Orval remembered the sadness and worry of that day, and seeing their Grandpa so sad. They said it was the saddest day of their lives.

Lloyd Sorter always took good care of his mother, Minnie. He built up the farm to 450 acres, raising grain, grass seed, hay, a few sheep, cattle and a dairy herd, becoming one of the leading farmers in the area. He invented a machine to help clear the fields of the many rocks that kept rising to the surface. He kept busy, inventing things of that sort, like a set of saw-horses that can be disassembled and stored flat.

Lloyd and Aunt Minnie were included in the Mortensen family gatherings. Most Sundays and holidays and other family gatherings were spent at the Mortensen home.

Aunt Minnie, with her twinkling eyes, was loved by everyone who met her. She was everyone's idea of a perfect aunt, remembering everyone's birthday, family and neighbors alike. (People who lived miles away were still "neighbors.") The family was amazed how she remembered all those dates.

In the times when people used kerosene lamps for light in their homes, fires were a constant threat. Aunt Minnie was so afraid of fires that she'd keep the lamp wick so low the house would be very dimly lit. She was troubled with aching feet and had a hard time getting comfortable shoes. She'd pad around the house wearing galoshes, which did not help the problem at all.

She never had a bad word for anyone, but when Lloyd bought her a TV set, she began to watch wrestling. She'd get so incensed when the bad guys got too mean with the good guys; she wanted the good guys to get just as mean to the bad guys.

ꟈ

The Sorter Family: An Epilogue: In the fall of 1952 Orval drove to Oregon, bringing his parents and Aunt Minnie Sorter to visit. She and her sister Julia could not get over the sight of so much fruit going to waste, like apples left on the ground in the farm yards. We'd finished harvesting our evergreen berry crop, but berries were left on the vines—not enough left to make it profitable for the berry co-op to buy them. And evergreen blackberries are not the most flavorful to preserve. Earlier in the summer we had harvested a crop of Marion blackberries, which are much more flavorful; I'd made jelly and pies, and froze enough berries for winter's use, so I did not intend to use the left-over evergreens. But for people from northern Minnesota, where there was such a shortage of fresh fruit, this was very hard to understand.

While the family visited us, we took them to the coast for a day. On the way we stopped at a rest area. While walking around, Ray noticed Aunt Minnie standing near a large old-growth Douglas fir tree with her arms stretched around it. He asked her what she was doing, and she said, "I'm measuring this tree so I can tell everyone back home how big the trees are here in Oregon."

For several years after, when we drive to the coast, we'd look for "Aunt Minnie's tree." For long after it was removed, I still looked for the site and remembered Aunt Minnie's visit.

In her later years Aunt Minnie had an operation for cancer, from which she recovered quite readily. Not long afterwards, in 1963, she was visiting distant relatives in southern Minnesota. When she started to leave, she thought she was opening the front door. She lost her balance, fell down the stairs and died instantly. Everyone around Wannaska mourned her passing, as did all the family in Oregon, who felt privileged to have known this remarkable woman.

Lloyd and Minnie Sorter, 1964

ℰ

Lloyd Sorter was very active in the Riverside Church in Wannaska. He made sets of light fixture that were still used in the church in 1996. He also participated in civic affairs. In his later years, Lloyd suffered a severe heart attack. After recovering, he was advised to sell his farm and move to a warmer climate. He came to Oregon and went to community college to study civil engineering. He did well with his studies, but because of his age could not get work.

Lloyd moved into the house next to ours that Ray built for his mother. He and Julia lived there for a few years, but then he developed cancer. He made the trip back to Minnesota to visit his father's family members, but upon his return he was so ill that he had to go to a nursing home. He suffered a great deal of pain, but conducted Bible studies with other patients. The nurses were awed with his ability to do this while so ill. In 1974 he went to meet the Lord, and the family mourned for him as if he had been their own brother.

ᘓ

Aunt Minnie was not a very good cook (she'd had no one to teach her), but she made good cookies. Anyone in the family who is served treats from her recipes recognizes them at once as "Aunt Minnie's cookies."

Aunt Minnie's Cookies

Beat together:
1 C butter or Imperial margarine
2 C sugar
4 eggs
1 teaspoon vanilla

Then add:
1 teaspoon soda in 1 tablespoon vinegar

Sift together and blend in:
4 C flour
1 teaspoon baking powder
1 teaspoon salt
1 teaspoon lemon flavor and peel
1 teaspoon nutmeg

Bake 10 minutes at 350°

℘

7: Mortensen Families in Later Years

Ray and Bennie Mortensen, Uncle Morten, Andrew Mortensen, Knudt Lee, and Lloyd Sorter – Lois peeking from window

The Knudt and Annie Mortensen Lee Family

Knudt Lee family
Top, left to right: Earl Lee, Bob Sattre and Sara Lee Sattre
Bottom: Knudt, Leland, Bernice, Annie Mortensen Lee, Madelyn

Annie and Knudt raised six children—two boys and four girls. I only met Leland, with his wife Audrine. I first met them when we visited Wannaska on furlough from the army, and then again when I visited after my Army discharge. I was invited to Aunt Annie's home for dinner one evening and was made to feel very much at home, though they were surprised to learn that Ray was married. Aunt Annie gave me a beautifully crocheted dresser scarf that I treasured for years.

When I last visited, Leland's son operated the farm and their daughter-in-law was post mistress and cared for Lee's Store.

During their lifetime in Wannaska, Knudt and Annie were leaders in the town, Knudt at the store and Annie with the church, school, and other places. Sometimes she was a bit overbearing, but she had a heart of gold, ready to help anyone who needed her. They passed away in 1944 and 1945.

The Clarence and Martha Mortensen Davis Family

Morten Davis, a cousin of Ray's, lived in Portland for many years and often visited family gatherings with Uncle Jens and Aunt Nettie. He enjoyed and talking about his aunts, uncles, grandparents, and cousins.

In about 1985, Morten's sisters Katie and Biddie, who live near Washington, D.C., came to visit him. Morten called Ray's brothers and sister in Oregon to come to his home in Portland to visit with them. Ray and his family had never met the girls before and wondered what they'd talk about. He had nothing to worry about–we all talked as if we'd known each other forever. There was no doubt they were Mortensens–they all have the Danish appearance, and their friendliness also seems to be an inherited gene.

The Morten and Hilda Oslund Mortensen Family

Morten and Hilda Mortensen family
Morten, Elmer, Lila, Hilda and Morriel

When I first met Uncle Morten and Aunt Hilda, they lived in Karlstadt, a few miles west of Wannaska, where Morten operated a grocery store and they lived in a house behind it. Before Karlstadt, Uncle Morten had worked in Lee's Store and then operated a grocery in Pencer.

When I was discharged from the army, Ray and I decided that I'd come back to Oregon and live with my parents until our baby was born. We thought Ray's army outfit would go overseas, and if they did, I'd be left all alone in Michigan. We thought I should visit his parents on the way West. Train or bus connections made the trip to Wannaska difficult. Ray figured the easiest way was for me to take the train from Battle Creek to Chicago, then to Minneapolis, and then another train from Minneapolis to Karlstadt. He thought his aunt and uncle could then drive me from Karlstadt to Wannaska. Ray wrote to Uncle Morten and Aunt Hilda about our plans, when I'd arrive—at about 6:00 a.m.

When I got off the train in Karlstadt, no one was anywhere to be seen. I wasn't too worried, so I walked about the train platform for a while. After an hour, I noticed Morten's name above the grocery store across from the train depot. I took my bags, walked to the house behind the store and knocked on the door. His aunt and uncle woke up, surprised to see me—they'd never met me before—and invited me in.

As Aunt Hilda began to prepare breakfast, Morten went to the post office. He brought back their mail, which included Ray's letter telling them of my arrival. We got acquainted over breakfast, and they drove me over to Wannaska, very pleased to do this for Ray and me. They told me how surprised they were when they learned of our marriage: they wouldn't have been more surprised if Orval (stationed in Greenland then) had written that he was marrying an Eskimo girl. Evidently Ray had not been interested in girls before going into the army.

When we arrived at Ray's home in Wannaska, Julia came to the car. She thought I was Morten's and Hilda's daughter Lila. She was also very surprised to learn I was there. Later that afternoon, Ray's letter to his parents arrived. In spite of the surprises, I was made to feel completely at home for the two-week visit before coming to Oregon.

When Orval was stationed with the Army in Greenland, mail came by ship. He got letters from three aunts at once, each saying, "We sure were surprised to learn Ray is getting married."

Morten Mortensen family
Top, left to right: Morriel, Eddie, Elmer
Bottom: Morten, Lila, Hilda

Hilda's and Morten's children were all grown and married when we first met. They had a daughter and three boys. One, Morriel, had died a couple of years earlier of anemia.

Morten and Hilda were well liked in Karlstadt. Hilda was a very good cook. Each time we made trips to Minnesota, we drove to Karlstadt. Each time we visited Hilda's home, she'd say how sorry she was not to have anything to serve us besides coffee. Before she finished bringing dishes out—flat bread, other kinds of bread or rolls (plain and cinnamon), cookies, fruit and so on—the table groaned with the weight of things she "didn't have to serve."

Hilda Oslund Mortensen in her kitchen

Aunt Hilda's Flatbread

2 C white flour
2 C whole wheat flour
1 C 100% bran cereal
1 teaspoon baking powder
1 teaspoon salt
1 teaspoon soda
1/2 C sugar
1/2 C shortening
1-1/2 C buttermilk (you may have to add a tiny bit more)

Knead dough good, then make it into a loaf. Let it stand for a couple hours. Then cut it and roll one piece and so on, until all is baked at 375° on baking sheets.

"I use one of those wheels that are fluted and run over it before I bake it. It is easy to break into pieces after it is baked" – Marie

The George and Christena Mortensen Johnson Family

George and Christena Johnson family
Top, left to right: Ellen, Pearl, Clarence, Edmond, Jack, Velma, Ethel
Bottom: Margaret, Christena, George, Doris

In 1958, our family took Jens and Nettie Mortensen with us on a trip to Minnesota. We first went to Iowa to visit with Aunt Christena and Uncle George (Christena was a sister to Jens and Andrew). They raised their family there on a very successful large farm, mostly raising corn and hogs. Uncle George passed in 1960 and Aunt Christena in 1979.

When we visited George and Christena in Iowa, they drove us into the country to the small Danish Lutheran church that Grandpa and Grandma Mortensen had attended. The congregation joined with other small churches to form a larger church in town. When they disbanded, they left the Communion service, hymnals, and altar equipment in place. It looked as if a service had been disturbed, even though years had passed since services were held there, other than an occasional funeral for an older member. Amazingly, no vandalism had occurred.

The Chris Hardland and Hannah Mortensen Hardland Family

In Mortensen kitchen at Golden Anniversary
Left couple: Hannah and Chris Hardland
Right couple: Julia and Andrew Mortensen
Cupboard in back is from Grandpa and Grandma Mortensen's shivaree.

On our trips home to Oregon from Minnesota, we always stopped in Petersburg, North Dakota, to visit Uncle Chris and Aunt Hannah Hardland (Andrew's sister). Uncle Chris operated a grocery store there. When Hannah married Chris, he was a widower with two young children. Eventually four more children were added to the family.

When Ray was young, the Hardlands visited Wannaska at least once a year, which was a joyous time. Uncle Chris always talked to the children as if they were grown up, never talking down to them, and Uncle Chris had a very good sense of humor.

Once when Chris and Hannah were visiting Jens and Nettie in Oregon, Jens's cherry tree was filled with ripe cherries. Jens hadn't sprayed the tree, so the cherries were wormy. One morning Jens discovered Uncle Chris in the tree, eating the cherries. Jens told Chris he shouldn't eat them, and why. Chris, living in North Dakota where there's a limited supply of fresh fruit, kept on eating.

Chris said, "When I eat cherries, the worms have to look out for themselves."

When Ray's parents celebrated their Golden Wedding anniversary, Uncle Chris and Aunt Hannah were there, too. They'd been best man and matron of honor at Andrew's and Julia's wedding. I could feel the love that Ray had for them.

One of the Hardland cousins, Clarence, and his wife, lived near Oregon City for many years and were included in family get-togethers. Another Hardland cousin lived for many years in Alaska, hunting and trapping. Ray envied this cousin's way of living and would have liked to try it. In later years, this cousin moved to Arizona and has since passed on. Uncle Chris died in 1960 and Aunt Hannah in 1981.

The Jens and Nettie Reed Mortensen Family

Uncle Jens was a butter-maker at the Land O'Lakes Creamery in Wannaska in the early 1920s and also at another small town nearby. He met Antoinette "Nettie" Reed from Badger, and they married.

Uncle Jens and Aunt Nettie moved to Oregon in 1923 with a young son, Odell. They lived on several farms, but the Willamette Valley has a few places where the soil is not especially good for row crops and fruit farming. They just happened to try to farm on a couple of them, with poor results. They finally settled on a farm of several acres outside of Aurora (about 20 miles south of Portland) and began to raise hops. By then they had a girl, Lucille, and two other boys, Bud (Jerome) and Harold. The Depression was hard for farms in Oregon also, so the family had to struggle to make a living.

The Jens Mortensen family
Top, left to right: Harold, Odell, Jerome (Bud)
Bottom: Nettie, Lucille, Jens

In the 1930s, Ray went to visit his Uncle Jens and Aunt Nettie near Aurora, Oregon. His cousin Morriel was also visiting—a happy, enthusiastic person who everyone liked. While there, Morriel had another spell with his incurable anemia problem. He kept losing red blood cells and needed a blood transfusion. Ray had the correct blood type to help his cousin. He described how pale Morriel's coloring was before receiving blood and how rapidly the color returned afterwards. Morriel lived just a few more years, and the family felt such a deep loss when he died.

ꝏ

When Ray worked in Portland in 1940, he visited his aunt and uncle in Aurora on weekends quite often. One beautiful Sunday morning, December 7, 1941, Ray and the family were sitting at the table drinking coffee and talking, when someone said, "Did you hear what the radio announcer just said? Pearl Harbor is being attacked!"

That day brought about a change in everyone's life. Bud joined the merchant marines. Harold joined the Coast Guard. Odell had vision impairment, so he wasn't eligible for military service; however, he worked at a ship-building company in Portland, and also helped his father care for their hops.

Hop pickers, Aurora, Oregon, 1930s
Top, left to right: Morriel Mortensen, Lucille, Nettie (partially hidden), Jerome, Harold, and Odell. Front: Jens Mortensen

Ray's cousins in Aurora were close to each other in age, so they socialized together a lot. Lucille's boyfriend, Clifford Rappé (whom she later married and who served in the Navy) had a sister, Naomi. In summer 1942, Ray's brother Bennie came out to Oregon to visit his relatives for a few days, where he met Naomi. When he had to report for duty with the Marine Corps, he said, "Here I've just met a nice girl, and I have to leave." When Bennie returned from the service, they were married soon afterwards.

ꙮ

After the war, Ray and I returned to Portland. We visited Jens's family in Aurora often. Our little boy was about 20 months old then. Jens and Nettie had three or four granddaughters, but no grandsons yet, so Michael received a lot of attention. We helped pick hops during the fall of 1946, since Ray hadn't found a good job yet. Even after he did get work, Ray really wanted to find a farm. In 1948 Uncle Jens found a ten-acre farm for sale just a couple of miles from his farm. We looked and decided we'd buy it.

So we became involved with Uncle Jens's family holidays and baby-showers and other events. Jens and Nettie included their daughters-in-law and my mother and stepfather as part of their family. They became very close to our family, taking part of the place of Ray's parents as grandparents, because of the distance between Oregon and Minnesota.

Jens's health was not good. He had an ulcer operation not many years before I met him and never fully recovered. He worried about things a lot, and that probably contributed to his discomfort. When we visited some evenings, Jens would be resting after dinner, but he'd sit up and begin to talk about different things going on, and soon seemed to forget about not feeling well. He carried notes about his farming activities in his overall bib pocket. When he held little children on his lap, they'd try to take the notes out of his pocket. He'd gently put back the notes and say, "No, those are Grandpa's."

Jens had the typical Mortensen habit of teasing, Nettie being the one teased most often. She'd always respond with, "Oh, Jens," and blush. Before she married Jens, Nettie was a schoolteacher in Greenbush, and at one time had Kaukaugeesik in her classroom. She never had much training in cooking at home, and as a result learning to cook was a bit difficult for her. She told me that many times as she learned to bake bread, she'd bury her failures in the garden, rather than face the teasing she knew would come. Eventually she became quite a good cook. Nettie was a very understanding person with whom one could confide any problem one might have.

Though they've been gone from us for several years, when our family has a party, someone says, "Aunt Nettie and Uncle Jens should be here."

Nettie and Jens Mortensen, 1960s

ꕤ

Aunt Nettie's Apple Crisp
8 apples, peeled and slides
1/2 C water (or less) added into baking pan
1/2 teaspoon cinnamon
Sift together:
1-1/2 C flour
3/4 C sugar (can be part brown sugar)
Cut into flour mix:
1/2 C margarine or butter
Spread mixture over top of apples.
Bake in moderate oven until tender (350° – 45 minutes).

The Blanchard and Marie Mortensen Hunking Family

In the Jens Mortensen hop yard, 1940s
From left: Marie Mortensen Hunking, Uncle Jens, Harold Mortensen, Bennie Mortensen, Art Johnson

Aunt Marie (Andrew's youngest sister) and Uncle Blanchard Hunking lived in North Dakota. Aunt Marie made several visits to Oregon while we were on our farm. She liked to travel by bus to visit her children who lived at different places, and she stopped off in Oregon to visit with her brother Jens before continuing on to California to visit her daughter. Aunt Marie passed on in 1975.

In 1991, I finally met one of Marie's daughters. We visited her and her daughter in Placerville, California. Lorrayne and her daughter Judy showed us all around the area, mostly the historical sites of the 1849 Gold Rush. Our visit with Lorrayne and Judy was a very enjoyable one for both Ray and me.

The Andrew Mortensen Family

Andrew Mortensen family, early 1940s
Back, left to right: Mildred, Ray, Orval, Bennie, Ardythe
Front, left to right: Andrew, Lois, Julia

When Ray's father Andrew retired from active farming, he engaged in activities that he hadn't time for when he was farming. He did more gardening, planting raspberries and small trees. We brought out a spruce seedling he tended and planted it in our yard in Hubbard.

Andrew often went fishing. One day he planned to finish planting potatoes in the garden. As he came out to the field, with his arms full of the rest of the potatoes to be planted, a neighbor, Sam Erickson, drove into the driveway and said, "Andrew, let's go fishing."

As Orval tells the story, Andrew looked down at his arm-full of potatoes and the row where he intended to plant them. He dropped the potatoes and said, "Let's go." This was so different from Andrew's former habits, when work always came before fun.

Andrew, Julia, and Lois came to Oregon for a visit when we lived in Portland after WWII. Where we lived, we could approach the house from four different directions, on different roads. We'd be driving with Andrew and arriving close to our street, when Ray would tease his father, asking if he knew where he was. Andrew sighed. "I haven't known where I was since I got off the train." The hills were a bother to people like Andrew who lived where the land was flat.

In 1968, on Andrew's last trip to Oregon, he realized a life-long ambition, to go fishing in the Pacific Ocean and catch a salmon. He went with his brother Jens and caught quite a large salmon, which they had canned. Andrew carried that package of fish proudly on the train as he and Julia returned home to Minnesota.

ꟹ

Andrew and Julia celebrated their Golden Wedding Anniversary in 1964, with most of the family there to celebrate with them. It was a joyous day for everyone to see two people so happy with each other for such a long time.

Riverside Congregation – Mortensen Golden Wedding Celebration
Andrew and Julia Mortensen center front
Minnie Sorter, fourth from left, first row
Leland Lee, third from left, second row from the top
Mildred and Russell Simmons,
eighth and ninth from left, second row from top
Lloyd Sorter, top row, standing just below the man with a baby

Later Andrew developed cancer, and the family in Oregon went back to be with him. He rallied but had to go to Minneapolis for further tests and treatment. I went to Minneapolis to aid Julia in getting a room near the hospital. It was soon evident that Andrew was not going to get well. One day as we were leaving him for a while, Julia leaned over Andrew and whispered, "I love you."

ꝏ

By 1996, when I spent time writing this, Wannaska had changed a bit in the half-century since Ray left. Lee's Store was still operating, and there was a service station, a garage, and a lunch room. The school still was operating, and the church was very active. Leland Lee's family was all of the descendants of Jens and Ellen Mortensen left in town, though Mildred Mortensen Simmons lived a few miles south of town.

But oh, the memories that linger on.

—Marjorie Mortensen, 1996

ꝏ

ꝏ

APPENDIX

Mortensen-Olson Family History

This information describes Jens and Ellen Mortensen's families of origin, much of it from a family tree authored by Madelyn Lee Glenn in the 1930s, based on information received from Annie Mortensen Lee. Other information was provided from Ray Mortensen, Mildred Mortensen Simmons, and other members of the Mortensen family. More details can be found at http://chrisman.org/pedigree/out8.htm

The Peder Madsen and Maren Nielsen Family

Peder Madsen (~1678–1736) married **Maren Nielsen** (~1682) in Odense County, Denmark. Their children:

MADS PEDERSEN (d. 1812)
Niels Lang
Inge Lang (d. 1704)
Inge Lang
Hans Lang
Anna Lang
Hans Lang
Anna Lang (d. 1785)
Hans

The Mads Pedersen and Maren Hansdatter Family

Mads Pedersen (d.1812) married **Maren Hansdatter** (1729–1809) in Odense County, Denmark. Their children:

Hans
Maren (1751)
Peder (1754)
Jens (d. 1822)
Daniel (d. 1823)
Maren (d. 1763)
Anne Margrethe
Marie Elizabeth (d.1788)
MORTEN ESBEN MADSEN (d. 1812)

The Morten Esben Madsen and Kirsten Jespersdater Family

Morten Esben Madsen (d. 1812) married **Kirsten Jespersdater** (d. 1820) in Denmark in 1787. She was the daughter of **Jesper Larsen and Mette Olesdatter**, and the granddaughter of **Lauritz Hansen and Karen Jespersen** of Odense County. Their child:

MORTEN MORTENSEN

The Morten Mortensen and Ane Larsdatter Family

Morten Mortensen (1788–1860), a day laborer, married **Ane Marie Larsdatter** (1788–1853) in 1814 in the Skovby Distrist in Odense County, Denmark. She was the daughter of **Lars and Maren Larsen**, and the granddaughter of **Jens Jensen and Anne Laursen**. Their children:

- Mette Marie Mortensdatter, m. Jens Madsen (1809)
  - Karin Marie Jensdatter (1836)
  - Morten (1839)
  - Anne Marie (1841)
  - Maren Kirstine Jensdatter (1844)
  - Jens (1847)
  - Mads (1850)
  - Rassmus (1853)
- Lars (d. 1839)
- Niels (1823)
- MORTEN MORTENSEN (1820)
- Jens (d. 1845)
- Maren Kirstine

The Morten Mortensen and Johanne Jorgensdatter Family

Morten Mortensen, a farmer, was born in 1820 in Skovby Parish, Skovby District in Odense County, Denmark. Morten married **Johanne Marie Jorgensdatter** (~1827) in 1844 in Asperup, Odense County. She was the daughter of **Jorgen Rasmussen** and **Anne Frederiksdatter**, and the granddaughter of Rasmus Hansen and Johanne Jensen. Their children:

- Lauritz or Lars (1848)
- Ane Marie (1850), m. Thimpson
  - Lauritz
  - Hannah
  - Mathilda
- JENS M. MORTENSEN (1851)
- Maren Kirsten "Krystan" (1853)

The Morten Mortensen and Johanne Jorgensdatter Family, continued

Stena
- Nils and 1 other unnamed son

Jorgine ("Gena"), m. Chris Olson (a tailor; Eugene, OR)
- Martin
- Tilla
- Hannah
- Hannah
- Mattie

Ane, m. Hans Christian

Morten m. Stena (settled in Iowa)
- Hannah, m. Beck Larson
- Martin
- Clara
- Ernest (twin with Arnold)
- Arnold
- 2 other unnamed children

Jess (1869), m. Clara May Stephenson (1886)
- Hanne Mary (1907)
- 2 unnamed sons

Krystan

The Jens M. Mortensen and Ellen Marie Jensen Family

Jens M. Mortensen (September 9, 1851; October 10, 1944) married **Ellen Marie Jensen** (March 20 1854; February 18, 1941) on November 16, 1879 at Grindsted Parish, Slavs District, Ribe County, Denmark. The five oldest children were born and baptized in Grindsted, Denmark, and the three younger children were born and baptized at Dunlap, Iowa. Their children:

Annie
Martha
Morten
Christena
Andrew
Hannah
Jens
Marie

Details of these children's families in the following section.

Ellen Marie Jensen Mortensen's Parents

Ellen Jensen was the daughter of **Jens Anderson** and **Ane Andersdatter**, who died in early 1920s, well over 100 years of age. Their children:

Krystan, m. Dorothea
Nil
ELLEN MARIE – the only family member known to immigrate to America
Carl, m. Marie
Two sons named Andrew
Jens
Marie, m. Morten

Julia Olson Mortensen's Parents

Julia Olson was the daughter of **Jens Olson** and **Mary Bendicson**, who married in Fillmore County, Minnesota. Their children:

Minnie (1878), m. Abraham Sorter
    Archie
    Lloyd
Carl
Bennie
JULIA MATHILDA (1891), m. Andrew Jens Mortensen

The Children of Jens and Ellen Mortensen

1. Annie Mortensen

(1880–1945), m. **Knudt E. Lee**[10] (1876–1945). Their children:

SARAH ELLEN, m. Ingeman (Bob) Sattre (1894)
JENS EARL (1908), m. Clara Chilson (1917)
MADELYN IRENE (1911), m. Kirk Hinson (1909); m. James L. Glenn (1908)
LELAND MORRIS (1917), m. Audrine Petterson (1917)
  Sondra Ann, m. Dale Olsen
    Bradley Dale Olsen, m. Kristie Marie Joest
    Shan Renae
    Natalie Delray
    Nicole Lee
  Craig Leland, m. Bonnie Jean Mekash
    Stacie Ann
    Margo Jean
BERNICE (1919), m. Roe C. Blume (1916)
  Cara Lee, m. Francis William Lewis
    Samantha, m. Robert Woise
    William
    David
  Martha Ann, m. Harold Martinson
    Siri Anne
    Njol Erik
    Ane Maren
    1 unnamed son
  Eric, m. Valerie Whan
    Brad
    April

[10] Knudt Lee's genealogy is discussed at http://bit.ly/18Ix6Fr

2. Martha Mortensen

(1881–1941), m. **Clarence George Davis** (1882). Their children:

CATHERINE (1907), m. Ralph Aaron Cruze (1902)
Mary Catherine, m. Vernon Holyoke
Deborah Sue
Julie Lynn, m. Clifford Hyder
Ralph Aaron II, m. Rosita Schlessinger
Tracy Lynn
Ralph Aaron III
EDITH MAE (1909), m. Robert Edward Gardner (1909)
MORTEN JENSEN (1912), m. Ruth Roper
Morten Jerry, m. Sylvia Clark
Mark Jerald
Warren Clark
...*later* m. Lenore Cooper
Robert Sidney, m. Bonnie Kidd
Clarence George, m. Rebecca White
Morgan Jensen
... *later* m. Janet McKibben Jacobs (1910)
KATIE ADELIA (1915), m. Sidney Wendell Nelson (1901)
Barbara Ellen, m. Harry Lee Wheeler
John Wesley
Andrew Nelson
ELLANORE GERTRUDE (1919), m. Milton Alva Cramer (1908)
Hilton Alva, m. Ethel Joan Hymes
Selena Ann, m. Kevin Lantry
Joni Lyn
Agatha Michel
Milva Althea
Michael Davis, m. Mary Allison Seek
Sara Delia
Martha Adelia, m. John Ronald Manhollan
Donna Marie, m. Stephen Hawkins
John Ronald Jr.
Jeffrey Chris
Ellamore Ann, m. Charles Evans Jeffries
Edith Mae, m. Douglas Wayne Johnson
Douglas Wayne, Jr.
...*later* m. George James Bonebrake
Ashley Gorden
James Jacob

3. Morten Mortensen

(1884–1953), m. **Hilda Oslund** (1891). Their children:

MORRIEL ORLANDO (1910)
ELMER KENNETH (1912), m. Lorrayne Wollin (1927)
    John Kenneth
    Elaine Marie
LILA C. (1916), m. Caryl Vernon Winjum (1918)
    Gwendolyn Beth
    Janice Muriel
    Sandra Kay, m. Willard Varner
        Jason Winjum
    Joseph Caryl
    Patrice Ann, m. Romeo Heynes
        Jonathan Romeo
EDWIN JENS (1922); m Dorothea Frances Dennis (1921)
    Dennis Morriel
    Karen Ann, m. Randy Mixon
    Pamela Ann, m. Steve Farovich

4. Christena Mortensen

(1887–1979), m. **Jens George Johnson** (1886). Their children:

EDWIN HERMAN (1908), m. Lucille Jepson (1912)
    Nadine Lucille
    James George, m. Joan Price
        Joyce Lucille
        Joanne Lynne
        Jeffrey Edwin
    Everett Dale, m. June Santage
        Timothy James
        Stewart Douglas
        Michael Everett
        Brandon Thomas
    Edwin Harold, m. Karen Eide
        Traci Ann
        Todd Allen
        Scott David

The Christena Mortensen and George Johnson Family, continued

ELLEN MARIE (1910), m. Andrew Knoff (1901)
- Betty Ellen

JENS CLARENCE (1912), m. Alice Johnson (1911)
- Ruth Christine, m. James Chancy
  - Brian Charles
  - Kara Marie
  - Blair Edmunde
- William Charles

MARGARET (1914), m. Roy Flayharty (1910)
- Sally Jane, m. Jack Jones
  - Kathleen Anne
  - Jeffrey Mark
  - Scott Alan
  - Steven Michael
- Sandra Kay, m. Glenn Leathers
  - John Anthony
  - Jonathan Glenn
  - James Andrew
  - Benjamin Roy
  - Jessica Rae
- Ross Anthony, m. Virginia Winston
  - Wendy Renee, m. Jamie Batten

JOHN HENRY (1917), m. Margaret Peterson (1924)
- Barbara Ann, m. Robert Pabenau
- ... later m. James Lauser
- Roger Wayne, m. Karen Seeberltng
  - Roger Martin
  - Nathan James
- ... *later* m. Janine Rechler

PEARL SENA (1919), m. Philip O'Dowd (1915)
- Patricia Ann, m. Jeffrey Shahan
  - Timothy Shawn
  - Sandra Colleen
  - Pamela Christine
  - Renee Elizabeth
- Kathleen Joyce, m. Winston McColl
  - Heather Leigh
  - Courtney Ledgerwood
- Michael James, m. Nancy Fischer
- Joseph Philip

The Christena Mortensen and George Johnson Family, continued

- VELMA ANITA (1922), m. Russell Johnson
  - Kristine Belle, m. David Bank
    - Leslie Lynn
    - Ryanne Kristine
    - Jonathan David
    - Whitney Louise
  - Jeffrey Boice, m. Emily Bailey
    - Steven Russell
    - Jill Ann
  - Kim Dianne ETHEL CHRISTENA (1924)
- DORIS IRENE (1921), m. Earl Nelson
  - Karen Joy, m. James Belz
    - Steven Mark
    - Michael Scott
  - Cynthia Lee

5. Andrew Mortensen

(1889–1967), m. **Julia Mathilda Olson** (1891). Their children:

- RAY LEONARD (1915), m. Marjorie Louise Wright (1921)
  - Michael Ray, m. Lorrie D. Winters
    - Julia Louise, m. Daniel Rowan Ruble
      - Gideon
      - Kaya
    - Mikael Orval
    - Rebecca Anne Glaze
      - Amelia
  - Elizabeth Ann, m. Christopher Stewart
    - Jacyn Rebekah
  - ... *later* m. Gregory Pearson
    - Martha Emily
  - Laurie Ellen, m. Rodney Lee Andreas
    - Katherine Danielle, m. Jonathan Dettwyler
      - Dalles
      - Devon
      - Faith
      - Raymond
    - Keri Lee, m. Theron Covey
  - Sally Diane, m. William Robert Cady
    - William Joshua, m. Crystal Johnson
    - Robert Joseph Cady

The Ray and Marjorie Wright Mortensen Family, continued

- Christine Marie, m. David Daniel Snodderly
  - Mellissa Sue
  - Timothy James
    - Kyleigh
  - Jonathan, m. Meagan Smallwood
    - Caleb
- Andrew Jens, m. Jennifer Stull
  - Hannah
  - Jens

ORVAL HAROLD (1918), m. Ina Erickson Wierschke (1919)

- Robert John Wierschke, m. Diane Jean Hagge
- Scott Robert Wierschke

ARDYTHE ELLEN (1920), m. Clifford James Byron Fredrickson (1921)

- Lola Jean

BENNIE LEO (1922), m. Naomi Adeline Rappe (1926)

- Jacueline Kay, m. Richard Gary Rygh
  - Tammy Michelle
  - Julie Ann
- ...*later* m. John Monroe Willis
- Carol Ann, m. Bryn Glenn Rygh
  - Stephanie Marie
  - Jeffrey Bryan
- Douglas Lee, m. Gretchen Sue Root
  - Adrienne Lynn
  - Tucker Douglas
  - Hillary Anne
- Debbie Renee

MILDRED MARY (1927), m. Russell Elmor Simmons (1922)

- Sheryl Olivia, m. Richard Jay Gudvangen
  - Tristan Jay
    - Owen
- Scott Russell, m. Milly Pracher
- Jerry Andrew, m. Katherine Tobin
  - Jamie
  - Missy Preteau
    - Madison
    - Wyatt
  - David

The Andrew and Julia Mortensen Family, continued

LOIS CARROLL, m. Emrance Lavern Berger
- Cindy Rae, m. Michael Voves
  - John
  - Scott
- Vaughn Lavern, m. Pamela Burke
  - EmRance
  - Kyla

6. Hannah Mortensen

(1891–1981), m. **Chris Hardland** (1883). Their children:

EDWARD BERNARD (1915), m. Ruth Tripp (1910)

LEONARD SIGFUS (1917), m. Geraldine Stafford (1919)
- Catherine
- Chris Michel
- Susan, m. Steven Eugene Meador
  - Laura Elizabeth
- James Leo
- John Russell

HELEN (1919), m. Ernest Ranstrom (1899)
- Lyle, m. Laura
  - David
  - Jennifer
  - Michelle
- Beverly, m. Gary Mielke
  - Brian
  - Tommy
- James, m. Linda
  - James Jr.
  - Scott
- Leroy
- John
- Mary

MERLE EUGENE (1922), m. Margaret Pauline Davidson (1921)
- Michael Chris
- Rocky M.
- Danna Marie

Hannah Mortensen Hardland's Stepchildren

BEATRICE H. (1905), m. Miles Benz (1905)
- Lloyd M., m. Virginia
  - Monte James
  - Lisa
  - Larry Lloyd
  - Naomi
  - Marianne
  - Laura
  - Miles Edwin
- Marian J., m. Maynard Forness
  - Katherin
  - John
  - Patricia
- Vivian, m. Williah H. Boelk
  - Denise
  - Gaylen
  - Lori
  - Gary
- Leone, m. Dennis R. Kressin
  - Valarie
  - Vicki
- Carol, m. Leonard Waswick
  - Celeste
  - Deanne
  - Mark
  - Lynette
  - Paul
  - Steven

MARGRETE IRENE (1907), m. William Russell Nickerson (1901)
- Joan Loraine, m. Donald Lee Olsen
  - Nancy Dawn, m. Michael Martin
  - Sandra Lee, m. Richard Dijdzhtski
    - Jessica,
    - Emily
- William Lyle, m. Signe Troberg

CLARENCE SIDNEY (1909), m. Irene Margaret Berge (1914)

7. Jens Mortensen

(1894–1981), m. **Antoinette (Nettie) Bartlett Reed** (1892)
Their children:

ODELL (1918), m. Floy Eatherton (1921)
Marlene m. Charles Maillard
Kim
...*later* m. Ed Kennicut
Terri
LUCILLE (1921), m. Clifford Rappe (1916)
Linda, m. Leon Christian
Lonnie
Lucinda
Craig, m. Debbie Rice
Aislynn
Trent
Jessica
JEROME (BUD) (1924), m. Gladys Plymate (1925)
Vicki, m. Jim Adamson
Tracy
Brent
Lynn, m. Johh Hallind
Heidi
Boone, m. Sandi Whittkopp
Alexander
Todd
Kelly, m. Mark Gerstner
Angie
April
Tory
HAROLD (1925), m. Ellen Whitney (1926)
Sandy, m. Doug Crawford
Carla, m. Dwayne Brick
Tessa Renae
... *later* m. Paul Thorn
... *later* m. Riley Abbot
Ryan
Julie, m. Dan Evy
Larry, m. Carla Lineborger
Casey, m. Cindy Lee
Jeremy

8. Marie Mortensen

(1898–1974), m. **William Blanchard Hunking** (1896–1953)
Their children:

LEROY ALLEN (1920), m. Frances Meyers
  Arlyss Jean, m. Gary Lee Hamrick
    Christopher Lynn
    Angela Rene
    Stephanie Dawn
...*later* m. Margaret Lederman
  Paul Roy, m. Denise Laugherty
ELIZABETH LORRAINE (1922), m. Charles Lanbert Sheridan, Jr. (1921)
  Judith, m. Larry Sam Krattiger
    Douglas Steven, m. Brenda Sue Crumm
      Christopher Steven
    Jeffrey Charles
  Geraldine Rae, m. Peter Rogness
    Rebecca Lee
    Sarah Elizabeth
    David Allen
  Jacqueline Faye, m. Gerald Wayne Sutterfield
    Justin Hayne
    Joshua Arron
  Charles Lambert III, m. Gail Dahl
EUGENE HAROLD (1924–1960), m. Wanda Perkins
  Eugene Harold, Jr.
  William Blanchard
  Keith Ray
LORNA HELEN, m. Myron Hedrick Nysveen
  Tammi Lorna, m. Jeffrey Joseph McDonald
  Dirk Myron
  Shawn Eugene

ꟹ

About the Author

MARJORIE WRIGHT MORTENSEN grew up in Portland, Oregon. As an adult, her only extended sojourn out of Oregon was as a member of the U.S. Women's Army Corps.

Following her childhood in Oregon, she lived in Hubbard, Oregon from 1949 until her death in 2002. After the Army, she worked as a mother, farmer's wife, and city bookkeeper. She was an avid painter and friend to hundreds in her town and church.

She is also the author of *A Girl from Sellwood*—memories of her girlhood in Portland, Oregon in the 1920s.

ꝏ

About Jugum Press

Voices from History Series

Jugum Press, a small independent publisher, presents a series of historic monographs and memoirs, featuring personal stories about unique experiences living in America.

The *Voices from History* series is available at online stores—or request these books from your local bookseller.

A Boy from Wannaska
by Marjorie W. Mortensen

Sparkling tales of life in a tiny northern Minnesota town amidst first-generation Scandinavian immigrants in the early twentieth century.

A Girl from Sellwood
by Marjorie W. Mortensen

Memories of a childhood in Portland, Oregon, in the 1920s.

Journey Into Gold Country: Memories of a Forty-Niner
by Ralph Buckingham; foreword by Charles Barker

Three wild years in the California Gold Rush, remembered in tranquility sixty years later by a New England younger son of a youngest son who went to seek his fortune.

www.jugumpress.com

CPSIA information can be obtained
at www.ICGtesting.com
Printed in the USA
LVHW042311081020
668387LV00017B/2333